Eugene Lee-Hamilton

Gods, Saints & Men

Eugene Lee-Hamilton

Gods, Saints & Men

ISBN/EAN: 9783337335939

Printed in Europe, USA, Canada, Australia, Japan

Cover: Foto ©Lupo / pixelio.de

More available books at **www.hansebooks.com**

GODS, SAINTS, & MEN.

BY

EUGENE LEE-HAMILTON,
AUTHOR OF "POEMS AND TRANSCRIPTS."

WITH TEN FULL-PAGE ILLUSTRATIONS DESIGNED BY
ENRICO MAZZANTI.

LONDON:
W. SATCHELL & CO., 12 TAVISTOCK STREET,
COVENT GARDEN, W.C.
1880.

PREFACE.

THE stories treated in the following Poems have been obtained from various sources. One or two only can be found in books; the others have been picked up in conversation, or suggested by a mere word or a mere picture; thus the "Ring of St. Mark" was suggested by Giorgione's *Storm* in the Academy of Venice, the "Emperor on the Ledge" by the Martinswand near Innsbruck; while "the Death of the Duchess Isabella" is a development of a scene in Webster's "White Devil;" the "Fiddle and the Slipper" (the only one of these poems which does not appear for the first time, having been printed in the "*New Quarterly Magazine*" for July of last year,) embodies a mediæval legend which has wandered all over the continent, and which, first heard many years ago, with reference to a shrine in the Rhineland, and subsequently as a legend of Burgos Cathedral, I met last autumn in the rough ballads hawked about the town of Lucca on the festival of the Holy Face, and yet again in a half effaced giottesque fresco recently sawed from the wall of a Veronese palace. The "Rhyme of the Reeds" is a fragment of an Italian fairy tale of which I have forgotten the remainder: while "the Witness," the "Keys of the Convent" and the "Ride of Don Pedro," were told me by a friend from Granada. The "Last Love of Venus" is my own development of one of the legends of the Tannhäuser cycle collected or invented by Heinrich Heine; and the "Rival of Fallopius" is my own conception of a scene which may more than once have taken place in the sixteenth century, and which certain philanthropical men of science may perhaps regret not to see repeated in the nineteenth.

E. L. H.

July, 1880.

CONTENTS.

	PAGE
The Last Love of Venus,	1
The Fiddle and the Slipper,	31
The Rhyme of the Reeds,	50
The Ring of St. Mark,	57
The Emperor on the Ledge,	64
The Keys of the Convent,	73
The Bell Founder of Augsburg,	79
The Witness,	92
The Ride of Don Pedro,	105
The Impious Stone,	108
A Rival of Fallopius,	112
The Death of the Duchess Isabella,	123

THE LAST LOVE OF VENUS.

THE Gods of beauty and of gladness
Lived on; but exiled and in sadness.
Long since their last adorer's prayer
Had died upon the desert air,
And round their temple's shattered column,
The silence was complete and solemn.
In shirt of hair, the scourge in hand,
A thousand saints in every land
Usurped their high antique command.
The chant of monks, the parting knell
Upon the ear for ever fell;
Or else the savage clank of steel
As men stalked armed from head to heel.
Each radiant and immortal God
The lonely path of exile trod
In pale disguise; or had retreated
To distant shores, and lay secreted.
Thus in a mountain's deep recess,
In undiminished loveliness,
Dwelt Venus in the middle ages,
Decoying some stray knights and pages,

And cheering exile's endless leisure
With mortal loves and earthly pleasure.
Where loudest rose War's shriek and rattle,
Rallying the Paynim in the battle,
A strange knight-errant might be seen
Of superhuman strength and mien,
Whose vizor's closed and narrow bars
Concealed the dazzling face of Mars.
A few on some far distant sea,
Where adverse winds had made them roam,
Had seen the car of Neptune flee
At their approach across the foam,
With Tritons spouting in the breeze,
And green-haired Oceanides.
Disguised, Apollo sought the gloom
Of many a bare monastic room,
And like a sunbeam peeped and peered
At many a monk who nothing feared.
When they were copying after matins
Some lyric poet of the Latins,
He whispered softly in their ear:
Of worlds of beauty which had perished,
Of things divine no longer cherished,
Of sounds which men had loved to hear.

So lived the Gods, expecting ever
The happier days which followed never,

While all their bright dependent train
Had shape of imps and goblins ta'en:
The Fauns and Dryads changed themselves
Into queer wayward forest elves;
The Naiads lurked as spiteful Nixes
In sunless pools, or dreaded Pixies,
Who could assume a deadly beauty,
Could lure the Christian from his duty,
And while his earthly peace they stole,
Endangered his immortal soul.

I love the legends which relate
To these strange exiles and their fate;
Long since from high Olympus hurled,
And wandering through an altered world:
Bright forms of beauty which intrude
Mid times of stern and savage mood,
And hover o'er midæval gloom
Like flowers waving o'er a tomb.
I love to note their secret dealings
With mortals ever and anon,
When all was changed, thought, life and feeling,
And nature's votaries were gone.
I love in this prosaic day
 To watch, through fancy's rainbow portal,
The rapid loves of an immortal,
With one of merely human clay;

So gather round and let me tell
The strange adventure which befell
A Knight of that same Suabian band
Who left their northern mountain home,
When, to be crowned by Papal hand,
Imperial Otho came to Rome.

He was a youth of noble blood
Named Wolfram, whose o'er-dreamy mood
Earned him small love from other knights.
He cared not for their tales of fights,
He seldom in their converse shared,
Nor for their sports and revels cared.
They called him love-sick, for they knew
That he at home had said adieu
To one to whom he was betrothed.
He loved the thing which most they loathed.
He loved that soft Italian land,
He spoke its soft seductive tongue,
He loved the southern breeze which fanned
The vines which there in garlands hung.
But most of all young Wolfram cherished
Those Roman ruins, strange and vast,
Which vaguely spoke of greatness perished,
And of a far forgotten past;
Where self-sown flowers sought to deck
Each fragment of the mighty wreck.

The Last Love of Venus.

He loved to roam alone and linger
Where Time, with slow reluctant finger,
Was wiping gradually away
The splendours of the Cæsars' sway.

Not far from where the knights were quartered,
Beside the Tiber where they watered
Their glossy steeds at break of day,
Immense and lonely ruins lay:
Baths, temple, palace,—none I ween
Now knew what once their use had been.
The giant masses, crumbling slowly,
Like rocks, and yet not shapeless wholly,
Formed mighty courts, where none except
The lonely goat-herd ever stepped;
Where all around was verdure sighing,
Where columns in the grass were lying,
Where wild acanthus, strong and green,
Was round the marble leafage seen
Of shivered capital and frieze;
Where violets nodded in the breeze,
And half concealed the fragments fair
Of broken statues scattered there:
A rounded arm, or an upturned face
Still smiling on the lonely place.
While from this world of shattered marble
And new-born green rose up the warble

Of birds unnumbered, quick to sing
The praises of awakening spring.
Here, mid the rubbish and the flowers,
Would Wolfram linger many hours,
And often ask himself with wonder
Before those mighty arches yonder,
What strange and giant men were they
Who, in a long-forgotten day,
Had built such stout and lofty halls,
Compared with which his castle's walls,
Suspended like an eagle's nest
Upon his Suabian mountain's crest,
And which the foe had feared to scale,
Had seemed but insecure and frail;
And then his thoughts would wander home,
Far from this vast and crumbling Rome,
To where his sweet affianced bride
Sat, fair of hair and modest-eyed,
Awaiting with ill-hidden yearning
The happy time of his returning.

One day that Wolfram thus alone
Was roaming through this world of stone,
His eyes, all careless, chanced to fall
Upon an opening in the wall,
Half hidden by a waving screen
Of ivy and luxuriant green.

The Last Love of Venus.

He pushed the leaves aside and found
A passage leading under ground;
And soon was in a vaulted room,
Bare, spacious, and half-plunged in gloom,
Which led to many other halls,
Bare like itself, with frescoed walls.
All would in total gloom have slept
Had not the summer sunshine crept
Into one hall whose vault, more thin,
Seemed lately to have fallen in.
The pictured floors were dimly seen,
Inlaid with marbles white and green,
Where griffins battled, fierce of mien,
And mermen strange, whose curling tails
Were covered o'er with fishy scales,
While round each group a wreath of vine
With hanging grapes was made to twine.
O'er all these strange designs he passed
From hall to hall and reached the last;
It was a small and dome-shaped hall,
Where high upon a pedestal
A single marble statue stood,
Sole tenant of that solitude,
Who in the faint mysterious light
Looked down upon him cold and white.

A superstitious terror crept
O'er Wolfram's heart: he backward stept.

It was a statue, sure he felt,
To which the Christian ne'er had knelt;
One of those Pagan gods who stole
The peace of man's immortal soul;
One of the few intact, unbroken,
Of whom his friend, the Monk, had spoken;
One of those baleful ancient Gods,
Whom Jesus, after fearful odds,
Had banished from the face of earth,
And who, some said, were nought but devils
Who still at times held impious revels,
Mid scenes of strange unhallowed mirth.

Whiter and whiter seemed to loom
Her limbs of marble in the gloom,
No lanky saint, berobed and pure,
Such as in churches stand demure;
But one whose limbs were softly rounded,
Of beauty splendid and unbounded;
'Twas Venus such as from the wave,
She rose to conquer and enslave.
He knew her not, but felt her power,
And something made him shrink and cower,
For potent was the fiend indeed,
And well might to damnation lead.
If she should move? With thumping heart,
He quickly turned him to depart,

And, as he did so, felt a dread
Lest, if he only turned his head,
She should pursue with silent tread.

And yet, what made him linger near,
Despite his faith and pious fear?
What made him on the morrow seek
That chamber empty and antique;
That silent form which seemed to speak?
What made him tread with trembling feet
Once more that strange secure retreat,
In which for half a thousand years
No step had ventured to disturb
A godess potent and superb?

And through her strong and subtle power,
He lingered daily many an hour,
There in the strange and lonely place,
Merely to look upon her face,
In which his eyes could only see
Inscrutable placidity.
How dull, how coarse, his northern bride
Seemed by that marble statue's side!
This was the effigy; but where
Was she whose image was so fair?
Where was the godess? Where was she,
Whose face must still more glorious be?

Had not the Monk distinctly said
The Gods were conquered—but not dead?
Then might she not be lurking near
To this her marble statue here?
The Monk had said that they were devils
Who held unhallowed midnight revels;
But if their shape was like to this,
To have from such a fiend one kiss
And then be damned, were boundless bliss!

So Wolfram thought, and time passed on,
Till came the Eve of good St. John.
The thousand bells of Christian Rome,
In solemn swing from every dome,
Had for the faithful scarce sufficed
To utter forth the praise of Christ.
In long black files, and two by two,
The Monks had crawled the cloisters through,
To chant with white and listless faces
The vespers in the holy places;
And well might Monk and Layman pray,
Upon that waning summer day,
For, on that eve beyond a doubt,
All evil spirits were about.
It was the eve on which, 'twas said,
The fallen Gods might raise their head,
Emerging from deep hidden mines

To haunt once more their ancient shrines;
The Virgin could not move a finger,
To save the wretches who might linger
Among the ruins—unhallowed haunts,
Where leering fiends with impious taunts
Derided Mother Church, and even
Sweet Mary's self, the Queen of Heaven.

All this the Knight had often heard,
But yet, though still his conscience feared,
A force, 'gainst which he strove in vain,
Led him to seek the ruins again,
Upon this balmy afternoon,
The longest of declining June.
The sun had set, and now reposed
All Nature, after fiery hours.
Sweet languid scents, as evening closed,
Rose up from all the drowsy flowers.
Upon a fallen column sitting,
Young Wolfram watched the first bats flitting.
A sudden yearning, vague and strange,
A sense of some great coming change,
Came o'er his heart, which now stood still,
And now beat high with sudden thrill.
Strange leafy rustles reached his ear,
Like whispered words too low to hear.
All round him waved that blood-red flower

Which, in Adonis' mortal hour,
First sprang, full-petall'd, from the ground,
Born of the drippings of his wound.
The nightingales began to wake
Each other with their rapid shake,
And like wee meteors, here and there
The fire-flies darted through the air.

It was a night for mighty Love
To visit Earth from spheres above;
And as the stars in deeper blue,
More brilliant and more numerous grew,
So did the ruins sweeter get,
And sweeter yet, and sweeter yet.
Each towering mass of Roman brick,
Beclad with ivy dark and thick,
Grew ghostly in the dusky light,
And mingled slowly with the night.
The nightingales their chorus hushed;
The breeze no more the verdure brushed;
And silence settled upon all,
Except, at whiles, the owlet's call.
But suddenly was heard to float
Across the night a wondrous note,
Which seemed at hand and yet remote,
Like human voices grandly blending,
But far all human tones transcending.

The strange and all-pervading sound
Appeared to Wolfram now to flow
From heights above, now from below,
And now to gird him all around.

SONG.

Lo, the still Powerful, though the Forbidden,
   Now is approaching: prepare, prepare;
Come from each lurking place, safe and hidden,
   Gods of the woods, and the streams, and the air!

Fairer she is than Men's loveliest daughters;
   When she approaches the air feels mirth;
Laughing run on the rejoicing waters;
   Gladness returns to the cheerless earth!

Round her all outlawed Divinities cluster;
   Many they be as they come in her train,
Strong, ever young, at her bidding they muster;
   Shapes long unseen are emerging again.

Wreaths for her bower the wood nymphs are weaving,
   Satyr and Faun again people the dusk,
Oak-prisoned Dryads the oak bark are cleaving,
   Lurking where roses are fragrant of musk.

When she revisits her fane that is shattered
   Every anemone lifteth its head ;
Long though the Gods have been hidden and scattered,
   Ne'er will they perish till Nature be dead.

———

   The chorus ceased, and for a space
   Deep silence reigned throughout the place ;
   But hark: a strange and distant strain
   Falls on his ear—and now again.
   Is't joyous music from afar
   Coming in gusts which fitful are?
   Is it a sound of hurrying feet
   Which many echoes now repeat?
   See, see, amid the ruins, out there,
   That bright and ever-growing glare
   As of a hundred torches' flare!

   He started up, while ever nearer
   The sounds approached, and ever clearer
   A sound of cymbals, pipes and drums
   Mixed with the shout "She comes! She comes!"
   Then, past a wild procession swept
   Of forms that bounded, danced and leapt,
   Divine and beauteous and fantastic,
   With gestures strange and orgiastic ;

The Last Love of Venus.

Who ever fair and ever young
Innumerable flowers flung
Upon the path of one by far
More fair than earthly beauties are,
And whom a strange tumultuous throng
Of frenzied votaries bore along
Enthroned upon a golden car.
And as the apparition fast
Before the dazzled Wolfram passed,
He saw, he felt—that she was one
With her whom he had loved in stone.
No time he had to pause or think,
No time to tremble or to shrink
Upon the Pagan revel's brink;
For he was whirled and swept away
By all those beings wild and gay;
Whither he knew not. When, at last
His wondering eyes around he cast
He stood in halls antique and vast.

Antique indeed, but cold no longer:
A rosy radiance filled them stronger
Than mortal eyes at first could bear,
While wondrous scents o'ercharged the air.
What unknown hands had unknown flowers
In garlands round each column bound?
What hands had stripped celestial bowers

To wreathe with buds the walls around?
What magic wand had summoned up
The bubbling waters, which again
Made music in each marble cup
Which had for ages thirsty lain?
What was this palace of delight,
Created in a single night?
And lo, like some bright ebbing flood,
The motley crowd, he knew not how,
Had ebbed and in a circle stood
Of which the centre he was now—
What could it mean? Was he a God
That all seemed waiting for his nod;
That faery forms thus gathered round him,
And with verbena garlands crowned him;
That on his path they flowers flung,
All trembling as he was and pale;
That in his praises hymns were sung
Which bade a new Adonis hail?

Through each bright hall, as Wolfram passed
Hailed like a God, and neared the last,
The one in which the Statue stood,
Why in his veins rushed fierce the blood,
Why thumped his heart and then stood still?
Why through his frame ran chill on chill?
One thought possessed him, one alone—

Would she be there, no more of stone?
Would she be there and breathe and move
With tongue to speak and heart to love?
Ah, well might Wolfram pause ere seeing
The worshipped, loved, and dreaded being,
For when she burst upon his sight
She seemed the focus of all light.
She stood upon the self-same spot:
Was she the Statue's self, or not?
Her glorious form was nude no more,
Strange iridescent robes she wore
By which she was completely draped,
Save where one rounded limb escaped,
Which in its rosiness might be
Of flame-illumined ivory.

The Goddess moved to meet the knight,
Who still stood dazzled at the sight
Of one so measurelessly fair,
And laid her hand upon his arm:
" Be welcome, Wolfram—Fear no harm,"
She said, so softly that her words
Like echoes of Æolian chords
Seemed floating through the scented air;
" Be welcome, Wolfram, child of clay,
Thou on whose heart a sunny ray
Has fallen in a gloomy world;

Thou whose fidelity has moved me;
Thou that hast worshipped and hast loved me,
Though long from brighter regions hurled,
Be welcome; lay all fear aside,
And with an exiled goddess bide."
"O Lady, whosoe'er thou be,"
The simple warrior answer made,
"If e'er young Wolfram's stainless blade
Can serve thee, or in some degree
Perchance contribute to redress
The wrongs of boundless loveliness;
Or if my life can serve thy cause,
Think not that I shall fear or pause,
And though I had to scale high Heaven,
Right gladly would my life be given."

The fallen Goddess eyed the youth
In whose blue eyes lay nought but truth,
And with a smile of sadness said,
As by the hand her guest she led:
"Alas, brave child, thy wish is vain,
Thy shining blade were weak indeed,
Where brighter falchions like a reed
Have hope betrayed and snapt in twain.
The friend of exiles, Time, alone
Can my usurping foes dethrone,
But come," she added, "and partake,

Before the red-winged morning break,
Of what, alas, can only be
An exile's hospitality."
And with these words she led her guest
Towards a couch-encircled board,
O'er which strange lamps their radiance poured,
And which with fruits and flowers was dressed,
Kissed into ripeness by a sun,
More fiercely amorous than the one
That sun-burnt Latian shepherds shun;
And many a massy golden cup
From mid the fruits and flowers gleamed,
And fare of savour yet undreamed,
Such as alone is heaped up
When mortals with immortals sup.
O happy and bewildered youth,
Is all around thee dream or truth?
Those ministering nymphs that hover
Around thee; o'er ambitious lover,
Those nymphs divine alone less fair,
Than thy immortal hostess there,
That feast, those flowers, and that light
Those couches which thy limbs invite,
That chorus of celestial voices,
Which near at hand thine ear rejoices;
Is't all a dream of false delight?

SONG.

One morn in the days that are olden,
    When young were mankind and the world,
The sea, dawn-illumined and golden,
    Was sleeping, by ripple uncurl'd.

A perfume of lemon was given
    To the air by the groves of the shore;
All sunny and silent the heaven;
    Not a sound of a song or an oar.

But suddenly over the waters,
    A music came floating along,
A music more sweet than the daughters
    Of man ever uttered in song.

O'er the face of the sea as it slumbered,
    Then ripple on ripple swept fast,
Which seemed like the kisses unnumber'd,
    Of Gods who invisible pass'd.

And Venus the snowy and scented
    From the watery mirror uprose,
Enthroned on a shell that was tinted
    Like the innermost leaf of a rose.

Through Nature and Man ran a quiver
   Announcing the Goddess's birth,
Who came to throw open for ever
   The flood-gates of Love upon Earth.

And Man saw how beauteous was Woman,
   And Woman how comely was Man,
Through all that was mortal and human
   A thrill of anxiety ran;

And all felt a sudden emotion:
   The worker in iron and gold,
The warrior, the netter of ocean,
   The merchant that bartered and sold.

The rustic who trudged heavy laden
   By a fount, empty hearted and dull,
Stopped short and looked long at the maiden
   As she stood till her pitcher was full;

Through his veins ran a thrill and a fire,
   A wish to possess her or die;
In her heart there up leapt a desire,
   Through her lips passed a word and a sigh.

And filled was Creation with kisses,
   With pantings and amorous sobs,
With pleasure from hidden abysses,
   With hopes and delusions and throbs;

All beauty was changed to perfection,
    And ugliness even was fair;
And hand-maids held kings in subjection,
    And conquered the conquerors were.

But how have the mortals requited
    The gift that was made to them then—
The gift that inflamed and delighted
    The thankless descendants of men?

Say, where is the smoke of her altar,
    And where the libations of wine,
And the prayers that the striplings would falter,
    And the wreaths that the maidens would twine?

Of the statues once raised in her honour
    How many unshattered remain?
And the hymns that heaped praises upon her,
    Will man ever breathe them again?

But though Venus is worshipped no longer,
    She lives, and her power men feel;
And Desire waxes stronger and stronger
    At the shrines of their saints as they kneel.

For though conquered and exiled from Heaven,
    Her reign upon earth is not done;
And the flame which she feeds rages even
    In the heart of the Monk and the Nun.

And after long months of dissembling,
   In spite of the thunders above,
They follow in fear and in trembling
   The mighty commandment of Love.

The Goddess took a myrtle wreath,
As scented as her own sweet breath,
And placed it on her lover's brow:
"By this, my own eternal sign,"
She said, "young Wolfram, thou art mine,
"Body and soul, for ever now."
And holding in her hand high up
A golden and o'er-brimming cup
Of Samian wine she bade him drink,
And pass Oblivion's fatal brink.
He took the glittering cup and drank,
And scarce had done so when he sank
Into the arms of Love and Sleep;—
Celestial slumber, not so deep
But that he felt each flaming kiss
And thrill of life-consuming bliss.

Then on his senses, as he slept,
After a while strange visions crept.
It seemed to him that through the air
He travelled with his goddess fair;

Upon a light and rosy car,
   Drawn by a hundred rustling doves,
To seek in lands unknown and far
   A harbour for eternal loves.
Above a sunny sea they flew,
Where, in clear depths of crystal blue,
She showed him Nereids scaly-tailed,
Who as they passed swam up and hailed,
And Tritons loud on sea-shells blowing,
With weedy beards and long locks flowing;
Who with the car kept rapid pace,
With gladness on each oozy face;
And as the airy chariot sped
The frightened clouds before it fled.
They passed o'er isles whose groves of palm
Were mirrored in the waters calm;
And next with faery speed they went
O'er tracts of sun-bathed continent,
Where cities fair, with temples white,
Glimmered beneath them in the light.
And then their dove-drawn car skimmed lightly
Where flowers decked the meadows brightly;
And over woods and woodland lawns,
By Satyrs peopled, and by Fauns,
Whose sunburnt limbs full length were laid
Where dots of sunshine pierced the shade,

"In all its golden age the world
Was thus beneath his eyes unfurled."

And who upstarted from their bed
To hail the dove-drawn car o'er-head;
And Wood-Nymphs white as Parian marble
Bathing with merry romp and scream
In shallows where the wood-birds' warble
Chimed with the babbling of the stream.
In all its golden age the world
Was thus beneath his eyes unfurled;
And she who showed it was more fair
Than all the beauty lavished there.

But o'er the scene there came a change,
A transformation passing strange:
The sun grew rayless, small and white,
And shed a pale and silvery light;
They still flew on; but underneath
Lay stretched a bare and moon-lit heath.
Nor did less wondrous change take place
In his companion's form and face:
Why grew her eye so dim and cold?
Why grew her cheek so thin and old?
As if each minute as it fled
Heaped years of ravage on her head?
Why grew so strangely curved her back?
Why took her voice so shrill a crack?
"Venus!" he cried, with outstretched arms,
As if to clutch the escaping charms,

"Venus, my Venus!"—but in vain
The desperate lover shrieked again.
O'er stock and stone, o'er dam and ditch,
He now was riding with a witch!
A prancing broomstick was their steed,
Which bore them on with magic speed.
No rosy doves of rustling feather,
But bats went with them winged with leather.
And as they passed each Christian steeple,
While soundly slept the Priest and people
The Witch unhooked the bells, and threw
Them in the fields o'er which they flew.

O monstrous Witch! O crazy flight!
O endless, endless, endless night!
Abhorring her he clasped her tight,
Afraid to fall from awful height.
"Hag! set me down!" he screamed in vain,
"O set me down!" he screamed again;
A cackling laugh was all he heard,
More eloquent than spoken word.
Northward their journey now seemed tending.
He saw no more the southern trees,
But dusky fir-trees now were bending
Beneath him in the chilly breeze
And soon they reached a mighty range
Of peaks which ghostly looked and strange;

"Their moon-projected shadow raced
Beneath them on the spotless waste."
Page 27.

Up ample valleys bright as day,
And gorges which in shadow lay,
They onward flew for ever higher,
On unseen wings that nought could tire:
Along the sharp and shining edges
Of walls of rock and narrow ledges,
And heard the roaring torrent flow
Unfathomably deep below;
Until they reached the plains where dwelt
Untrodden snows that ne'er might melt;
Their moon-projected shadow raced
Beneath them on the spotless waste.
"The Alps" he thought, and on they flew,
O'er frozen lakes and glaciers blue.
But when the mighty chain at last
In all its desert breadth was past,
And when the broom-stick flew again
O'er habitable hill and plain,
Familiar seemed the scene he scanned:
It was his own good Suabian land.
And high above the valley soon
He saw illumined by the moon
His father's castle, like a nest
Of eagles on a jagged crest.
Three times they circled round the towers
(What an abyss, Almighty Powers!)
Then for a window of the keep

The Witch made straight and bade him peep.
He looked into the well-known room:
A single lamp lit up the gloom.
There sat his granny, spinning slowly,
And, at her feet, in thought lost wholly,
Sat his Betrothed, whose candid brow
Unutterably sad looked now.
He called her name; she seemed to hear,
And raised her arms in sudden fear;
He saw no more: the broom-stick steed
Bore him away with dizzy speed;
And on and on, across the night,
He and the Witch pursued their flight.

Away, away o'er hill and vale;
Away, away, through the moonlight pale;
Away o'er fields by famine stricken;
And ever seemed their pace to quicken:
Past gabled towns whose towers quaint
Looked by the moon distinct yet faint,
And filled his heart with terror vague,
As if their silence meant the plague—
O monstrous Witch! O frantic race!
Will morn ne'er show its blessed face?
Then o'er a battle-field they sped,
Where lay the dying and the dead.

The Last Love of Venus.

The moon lit up their upturned faces,
Showed friends and foes in strange embraces;
Showed how the wounded tried to lift
The crushing weight, and posture shift;
Showed here and there a wounded horse,
With what remained of ebbing force,
Lift its long neck above the plain,
And try to rise, and sink again;
While, still afar, an evil howl
Told where the wolves began to prowl.
And suddenly the Witch with glee
Showed him a form which seemed to be
His Father's, near a heap of slain.
"Stop, stop!" he shrieked, "I know his face!"
But they pursued their crazy race
O'er plain and valley. But at last,
As o'er a lonely moor they passed,
She showed him on the scanty heather
A Witches' Sabbath: met together,
A hundred witches in a reel,
Danced back to back and heel to heel.
Some had from broom-sticks just alighted,
And many fiends he also sighted
Who to the witches with strange sport
Paid their abominable court.
A nameless horror filled his soul,
More potent than the hag's control.

He seized his sword, and with one stroke
Cut off her head,—and then awoke.

'Twas night no more, but early day.
With wondering eyes he looked around:
A lately fallen statue lay
Beside him, headless, on the ground;
The head—that head whose pagan beauty
Had lured him from his Christian duty,
Some paces further off had rolled.
And, by the legend we are told
That, lest in after years the youth
Should doubt his strange adventure's truth,
Or doubt the strong unhallowed power
Of her who loved him for an hour,
A wreath of myrtle in his sleep
Had on his brow been branded deep.

THE FIDDLE AND THE SLIPPER.

I.

IN an old town, which in the Rhine
    Reflects quaint mediæval towers,
    There stands a rich and holy shrine,
Famed far and wide for wondrous powers:
An image of the Virgin Mother,
More potent·far than any other;
Revered for strange and sudden healings
    By serf and burgess, priest and lord,
Ne'er thankless for a pilgrim's kneelings,
    And in the furthest lands adored.
The figure stands within the aisle
Of the immense Cathedral pile;
Where languid fumes of incense float,
And rolls the organ's solemn note;
Where gorgeous flecks of colour pass,
And kiss the stone through tinted glass:
A mild Madonna looking down
From underneath a starry crown,

And standing in an azure niche,
Behind a grating strange and rich.
So far, so good. But in this shrine
   There hangs just in the very middle,
Beside the effigy divine,
   A fiddle.
A Fiddle???
Each latest pilgrim shakes his head,
Whom pious steps have hither led,
   And questions all, with anxious face.
For 'tis indeed a puzzling riddle
Why such an object as a fiddle
Should be suspended in the middle
   Of such a very holy place.
But as I know, and as the story
Is greatly to the Virgin's glory,
I'll tell the legend unto you,
For whom 'tis peradventure new.

   Somewhere in the Middle Ages—:
That happy time of long-shanked pages,
Of troubadours and ladies fair,
With hawk on wrist and golden hair;
Of lovers' philtres, and of spells,
Of palmers with their cockle-shells,
Of tourneys, and of knightly prancings,
Of plagues and epileptic dancings,

Of monks and nuns with morbid cravings,
With visions and ecstatic ravings,
Of heretics' and witches' trials,
Of recantations and denials;
That kindly period which exhibits
So many forms of chains and gibbets,
Of thumbscrews, racks, and Spanish shoes
To alter men's religious views,
Or touch the heart of stingy Jews;
Those good old days so picturesque,
So hungry, pious, and grotesque—
In that same town beside the Rhine,
Where stands the venerable shrine,
A fiddler dwelt of humble fame,
And known as Nepomuk by name.
He earned but little at the best,
   For though his skill was far from middling,
Few in that city's bounds possessed
   A taste for piping or for fiddling.
But times were more than ever hard,
The very mice could find no lard;
A plague had lately swept the city,
And Famine showed but little pity.
The world had licked its platter clean,
And grew each day more pale and lean;
All had to borrow, steal, or beg.
The stork which stood upon one leg

Upon his dwelling's highest gable,
    Had brought to the musician's wife
More brats than he and she were able
    To furnish with the means of life.
The hearth was empty; all was bare,
    Their only visitor was Care;
Save when, through panes of bottle green,
    Grim Hunger's face would come and stare;
Or ever and anon was seen
    Upon the threshold blank Despair.

    But in the trouble of his life,
When even his devoted wife
Was all unable to console
The woe which weighed upon his soul,
The poor musician had a friend,
For ever ready to attend;
A friend to whom, when broken-hearted,
His every feeling he imparted,
Whose voice in vain was never heard,
A friend who with him hoped and feared;
By old companionship endeared;
Who, in his happier days of youth,
Before he felt Care's gnawing tooth,
Had at his joy exulted often,
And now could soothe, assuage, and soften;
A friend who stuck through thick and thin,

The Fiddle and the Slipper.

His comforter—his violin.
He was for ever fiddling found,
The less the food, the more the sound.
When, in that bitt'rest of all winters,
The floating ice in hoary splinters,
Would crash and crunch, and shake and shiver,
Against the pier-heads of the river;
And mighty blocks with creaks and cracks
Would leap upon each other's backs;
And when from gables, and from leads,
And rain-spouts shaped like dragons' heads,
Hung icicles a yard in length,
Resplendent in ephemeral strength:
Then ran the fingers, flew the bow,
Through mazes of unuttered woe;
Until the sweat, despite the cold,
Down from the player's forehead rolled.

One day when things looked blacker still,
(A child had died, his wife was ill,)
The poor musician had stolen out,
Scarce knowing what he was about:
Whether to seek some chance carousal,
Some christening feast, or some espousal,
At which to fiddle for a penny
(Feasts in the town were far from many);
Whether to supplicate or steal

For those at home a scanty meal;
Or whether every hope resign,
And end his misery in the Rhine;
It happened that the narrow street,
Chosen at random by the feet
Of the depressed and starving mortal,
Led past the great cathedral portal,
Where monkish sculptors, shorn and shaven,
Had nightmare scenes of yore engraven;
Where squatted imps, and goblins leered,
And apish faces grinned and jeered,
And fiends and dwarfs and creatures weird,
From every nook and corner peered;
Where rows of rigid Kings were seen,
Each with his lean and rigid Queen,
And mitred saints, all skin and bone,
Were rudely hewn in blackened stone.
The fiddler stopped and looked awhile;
   He felt an inner admonition,
   Far stronger than his own volition,
To enter that great Gothic pile.
   The nave and aisles in semi-light
   Seemed empty and deserted quite.
The sheaf-like pillars rose sublime,
   Sustaining lightly in the air
   A stony lace-work, past compare,
At heights where Fancy feared to climb.

Upon the tombs loomed cold and pale,
Recumbent in their coats of mail,
   The statues of once famous knights,
Who in the shade of arch and column,
And in the stillness deep and solemn,
   Seemed resting from forgotten fights.
The whole in tintless twilight lay,
Save here and there, where, far away,
   At some long pillared vista's close,
   A window like a luminous rose,
With blood-red petals, let a stream
Of crimson light the grey redeem.

The unknown impulse which had made
   The fiddler enter, led him on,
Through nave and transept, till it bade
   Him humbly kneel upon the stone
Before the rich and holy shrine,
Where stood the Virgin's form divine.
She stood behind the silver grating,
   Clad in a splendid jewelled robe,
As if for adoration waiting,
   Her feet upon an azure globe;
And from beneath her starry crown,
She looked so mildly, softly down;
She seemed to say, "I know thee well;
To me thy woes and troubles tell."

Was it his fancy? But he thought
That on her face a smile he caught.
Again! He thought her mantle rich
Had rustled in the azure niche!
He mumbled all the prayers he knew;
Half understood, and very few,
They served but badly to express
His utter misery and distress.
In his own words he tried to speak,
   But his own words his wish belied;
His heart was full, his tongue was weak,
   Upon his lips the accents died.
Then for his fiddle, as he knelt,
His hand mechanically felt.
At first the music sounded faint,
And like the moaning wind's complaint;
But as the player bolder grew,
From out his instrument he drew
A simple and pathetic air,
His truest, best, and highest prayer.
To her who, 'neath her starry crown,
Into all lowly hearts looked down,
He told his tale; and not in vain;
For lo, the image smiled again!
Again, against the azure globe,
He heard the rustling of her robe.
   Before his hand had wholly stopped,

"An iron gripe was round his wrist;
Upon his neck an iron fist;
There stood a grim, gigantic fellow,
A man at arms, in red and yellow."

Before his prayer had wholly ended,
Slightly her foot the saint extended,
   And through the bars, oh, joy unhoped,
   The Virgin's jewelled slipper dropped.

II.

He caught it up with wild delight,
And feasted on it soul and sight.
O beauteous gift! O wondrous token!
How clearly had not Heaven spoken!
   No more dark days; no more despair;
The strength of evil fate was broken!
   His life would now be bright and fair,
. He stood beneath the Virgin's care!
With ecstasies of faith and joy,
He looked upon the glittering toy;
Kissed it, pressed it to his heart,
And—gave a cry and sudden start.
An iron gripe was round his wrist;
Upon his neck an iron fist;
There stood a grim, gigantic fellow,
A man at arms, in red and yellow,
Whose words fell harshly on his ear,
And filled him with a hideous fear.
"So, so," he cried, "we've caught the thief!
At last the rat has come to grief!
Here, beadle! lend a hand. I feel

The fellow wringgling like an eel."
Up came the beadle and the priest;
The fiddler prayed to be released,
And, trembling, laboured to explain.
They listened not, 'twas all in vain.
"To steal," cried one, "the Virgin's slipper!
We'll hand him to the public whipper."
"No!" cried the priest, "this dreadful act
"Is sacrilege! he must be racked,
Till every bone he has is cracked."
They dragged him to the Marshal's dwelling,
Amid a mob with anger yelling;
And threats, and oaths, and kicks, and cuffs,
  Were in the Virgin's honour showered,
By more than fifty pious roughs,
  Upon the sacrilegious coward,
Who had just laid his impious hand
Upon the holiest in the land.
Before the Marshal and his crew,
The wretched Nepomuk again
All trembling laboured to explain
That all to miracle was due:
  That he had fiddled at the shrine,
  And that the effigy divine,
Had at his fiddling dropped her shoe;
But he was met with roars of laughter
That shook the very roof and rafter,

And after much enduring there
Was handed over to the Mayor;
Who called in haste his corporation,
And, after weighty consultation,
Declared that it was clearly shown
The case concerned the Church alone.
So late at night, he was at last
Into the Bishop's prison cast.

Now it so chanced that on that day
Just seven years had passed away
Since any one for Jesus' sake
Had been committed to the stake,—
An unaccountable vacation
Which hurt the Bishop's reputation;
It was a great and growing scandal,
Which gave his enemies a handle:
What wonder, when he did so little
  To honour Heaven and to please,
If Heaven sent the town no victual,
  But sent it famine and disease?
Too well this fact the bishop knew,
But what, alas! was he to do?
The heretics were now so sly
That 'twas mere waste of time to try
To set them traps; and as for wizards,
Who used to be as many as lizards,

His predecessor must have cast
Into the flames the very last.
For though he searched each nook and cranny,
He wholly failed to ferret any;
Nay, things had come to such a pitch
You couldn't even find a witch.
But suddenly, O hour of joy!
O golden day without alloy!
Behold the Heavens kindly send us
A case of sacrilege tremendous.
To touch the Virgin's jewelled shoe!
What next, good Lord, will Satan do?
Quick, heap the logs, and poke the fire!
Until the flames go shooting higher
Than yonder tall cathedral's spire,
And to the stake that's in the middle
We'll tie this fiddler and his fiddle!

But matters went not quite so fast,
For many an endless month was passed
(Indeed I think the months were seven)
Far from the gentle light of Heaven,
By that same fiddler, in a cell
Beneath the level of a well:
The home of darkness and of damp
Of squalor and of fettered cramp,
Where slimy waters oozed and trickled,

The Fiddle and the Slipper.

Where unseen crawling creatures tickled,
Where every limb did waste and shrink;
Where almost mind unlearned to think,
Where tongue unlearned to speak, and ear
Almost at last unlearned to hear,
Where almost eye unlearned to see,
Where moments were eternity;
Where Nightmare with her crazy train
Oft flitted in and out again,
Oft placed her cold mouth on his cheek,
And woke him up with sudden shriek.
For seven endless months he wasted,
Nor knew how long the time had lasted,
Nor why so little Death had hasted.
At last he was brought out, and learnt
That in a week he would be burnt;
That though his body turned to coal
He might rest pleased, for on the whole
'Twas mighty wholesome for his soul.
And then they told him if he wanted
To ask a boon before he died,
It would not surely be denied.

On Nepomuk's white altered face,
   A gleam of hope was seen to flit.
There was, he said, indeed a grace
   Which he would crave, and this was it—

Upon the dread and final day,
When he should be upon his way
To execution, might he play
Upon his fiddle at the shrine
Of Mary, Heaven's Queen Divine?
O Virgin, by whose image there,
He played too well his plaintive air,
Thou wilt not let thy fiddler die;
But from thy throne of stars on high,
Thou wilt forbid the act of shame!
   Once more thou'lt listen to his fiddle,
   And thou wilt snatch him from the middle
Of the devouring tongues of flame!

Slowly tolled the dying knell,
   With a dull ill-omened sound,
   While the long procession wound
Bent upon its work of hell.
Slowly went the monks and chanting,
   Cowled in brown, with sandalled feet,
In the shadow of the slanting
   Gables of the narrow street,
     "*Dies irae, dies illa*
     Solvet saeclum in favilla,
     Teste David cum Sibylla."
Then masked penitents with torches
   And two little holes for eyes,

Chanting how the hell-flame scorches,
   When the dead for judgment rise.
Then the priests with tapers marching,
   With the crucifix ahead:
Mighty burning, mighty parching,
   When the trump shall wake the dead.
   " Tuba mirum spargens sonum
   Per sepulchra regionum
   Coget omnes ante thronum."
Then the bones of great St. Gandolf
   (For the truth a mighty fighter),
Then the chains of sweet St. Pandolf,
   And the Bishop with his mitre;
Then the Virgin's stolen Slipper,
   Carried in a case of satin;
Then the Hangman and the Whipper,
   Chanting, too, in barbarous Latin.
   " Mors stupebit et natura
   Cum resurget creatura
   Judicanti responsura."
Then the Victim, walking slowly,
   Clad in sackcloth, bare of foot,
Seeming to be careless wholly
   Of the crowd's insulting hoot.
Fastened slackly round his middle
   Was a thick and knotted rope,
In his hand he held his fiddle,

Which was now his only hope.
    "Quid sum miser tunc dicturus?
    Quem patronum rogaturus?
    Cum vix justus sit securus?"
Then came monk, and knave, and varlet,
    Bearing fagots for the stake;
Men-at-arms, striped black and scarlet,
    Followed close for order's sake;
Then the emblems of the Passion,
    Hammer, Tweezers, Sponge, and Lance,
With the Coat of Seamless Fashion,
    And the Dice of evil chance.
    "Confutatis maledictis,
    Flammis acribus addictis
    Voca me cum benedictis."
Then the Guilds with all their banners,
    Weavers weak and Butchers strong,
Goldsmiths, Brewers, Coopers, Tanners,
    With apprentices in throng.
Then the crowd from all the quarters
    Poured into that single street,
Like to wild and turbid waters
    Which converge and roaring meet.

    The great procession had to pass
Through the cathedral to hear Mass;
Then, at the shrine within the aisle

The Fiddle and the Slipper.

The fiddler was to play awhile,
As had been promised and conceded,
Before the pious souls proceeded
Towards the city's largest square,
And burned him with his fiddle there.
So through the great cathedral porch
Passed priest with taper, monk with torch,
Into the shade of arch and column
Where echo made the chant more solemn,
And where the stain'd glass windows threw
Their wondrous gleams of many a hue.
There Nepomuk at last was brought
To that same shrine his feet had sought:
Where in her pointed azure niche,
Adorned with jewels rare and rich,
Stood Our Lady looking down
From underneath her starry crown.
They bade him fiddle, and if Heaven
Should give a sign, he'd be forgiven.
Now fiddle, fiddler, for thy life,
For worse than water, rope, or knife,
Is what awaits thee if thou fail
To move that Virgin's image pale!

He grasped his bow. Oh, piteous sight,
To see his lamentable plight!
His feet were bleeding from the stones;

The dungeon chains, worn day and night,
Had eaten to his very bones;
His lately shackled hands were numb,
No sound would from the fiddle come;
The faithless instrument was dumb!
He tried again, the cold sweat now
Stood in big drops upon his brow;
He tried again, a feeble whine
Was all 'twould utter at the shrine;
Then screams of laughter, spite the place,
Nor pity on a single face.
The Bishop swore with joy malicious,
The fiddler's tune was too delicious;
Was ever such a rare thing seen
As that most comic fiddler's mien?
But look! but look! why stops the mirth?
What to such silence can give birth?
"She moves! she moves!" runs through the crowd;
" She moves!" the Bishop cries aloud.
She moved, indeed: her pearly robe
Is rustling on the azure globe;
The statue with those features mild
Has on the fiddler surely smiled.
A mighty cry of wonder rends
The startled air, and for awhile
Wakes all the echoes of the aisle;
For lo, the effigy extends

Slightly her foot, in sight of all,
And lets the other slipper fall.

  Thus he was saved, and lived to tell
His children's sons how all befell;
Nor did his pains go unrewarded,
For he was made—so 'tis recorded—
Cathedral organist-in-chief,
With free supplies of bread and beef;
And when at last his days were ended,
His fellow-citizens suspended
Within the shrine, just in the middle,
His fiddle.

THE RHYME OF THE REEDS.

IN a Sicilian mountain-circled plain,
    Where fertile fields now long have
        fallow lain,
And clumps of reeds replace the ousted grain,
    See how the reeds are waving.

May still be seen upon a little steep,
Beclad with ivy and with flowers that creep,
The blackened remnants of a Norman keep.
    Hark how the wind is sighing.

Around each crumbling wall and shattered tower
The invading reeds have undisputed power.
    See how they all are waving.

It was a stately castle in its day,
Before the Norman rule had passed away.
    Hark how the wind is sighing.

The Rhyme of the Reeds.

Within its walls there dwelt two noble brothers,
Unlike as night and day, of different mothers.
    See how the reeds are waving.

The elder dark as Cain, with locks of sable,
The younger golden-haired, as fair as Abel.
    List how the wind is sighing.

One Bohemund, the other Berengar;
Their father's land extended wide and far,
Count Roger was his name, far-famed in war.
    See how the reeds are waving.

Both loved one girl; and she her heart had given
To Berengar; the choice was ne'er forgiven;
    List how the wind is moaning.

Thenceforth his brother cherished secret hate,
A hate as deadly as his love was great.
    Hark how the reeds are rustling.

As through a savage tract the brothers rode
One day alone, and far from men's abode,
    Where there were reeds high-waving.

Dark Bohemund, a traitorous weapon drew,
And, from behind, his fair-haired brother slew;
    Hark how the wind is moaning.

And like a thief, by guilt and terror hurried,
With trembling hand the blood-stained corpse he buried,
Among the pale green reeds erect and serried,
Gently around him waving.

At every sound he stopped in sudden fear,
Or heard a step, or thought a voice to hear,
Only the breeze was sighing.

While riderless and breathless, white with foam,
The frightened courser sought his distant home,
Roughly the reeds down-crushing.

None saw the deed: all took the murderer's word
That Berengar had perished in a ford,
Where the high reeds were waving.

With Spring's return, above the lonely grave
Young reeds sprang up to rustle and to wave,
There when the wind was sighing.

No step approached; no sound the silence broke
Save when, at eve, the distant bull-frog woke,
And, in the dusk, set up his patient croak,
Where the high reeds were waving.

"One day in autumn when the reeds were ripe,
He felt a whim to make a sylvan pipe."

Page 53.

The Rhyme of the Reeds.

At last, one day a goatherd brought his goats,
His horned and bearded goats, with shaggy coats,
    Where the high reeds were rustling.

A gentle lad who came each break of day,
And who at sunset went his homeward way.
    List how the breeze is sighing.

One day in autumn when the reeds were ripe,
He felt a whim to make a sylvan pipe.
    Hark how the reeds are rustling.

A pleasant hour upon the work he spent;
He notched the holes, he neatly cut the vent,
And trimmed the rustic instrument.
    See how the reeds are waving.

But scarce it touched his lips, than turning pale,
He let it drop in terror, for the frail
And slender pipe gave out a human wail,
    Low as the wind that's moaning.

He tried again, and lo, a spoken word,
Distinct though soft, the trembling lad now heard,
    There mid the reeds high waving.

" Sell all thy goats, and with this pipe of reed,
Across the world from hearth to hearth proceed,
So shalt thou prosper and avenge the deed.
    List how the wind is moaning."

So spake it thrice: he did as he was bid,
He sold his goats, he sold each bleating kid.
    See how the reeds are waving.

The magic reed-pipe spoke for rich and poor,
It knew the secret both of lord and boor.
    List how the wind is moaning.

Great were the goat-herd's gains, and like a flame
From place to place ran on the reed pipe's fame,
    Fast as the whirlwind speeding.

He reached a castle where a mighty crowd
Of guests were met, and revelry was loud,
While on the wall Count Roger's banner proud,
    High in the breeze was waving.

It was a nuptial feast, where side by side,
Sat Bohemund the bridegroom, and his bride,
Who once had been the bride of him who died
    Where the high reeds are waving.

The Rhyme of the Reeds.

With loud applause the lad was ushered in,
And old Count Roger cried above the din,
'Tis Bohemund, the Bridegroom must begin.
   Hark how the breeze is sighing.

He seemed unwilling, but obeyed at last,
And through the crowd a hush of wonder passed,
   Just as when reeds are rustling.

He took the reed-pipe from the lad and blew;
But as he did so, pale as death he grew,
For from the pipe, there came a voice he knew,
   Sad as the wind that's sighing.

He writhed in vain; in vain he tried to stay
His fatal breath; the pipe would have its way;
The hand of God was forcing him to play.
   Look how the reeds are waving.

"Where many reeds are waving tall and serried,
Was Berengar from life and sunshine hurried,
By his own brother's hand, and lieth buried.
   List how the wind is sighing."

From every mouth loud execrations burst,
But old Count Roger neither wept nor cursed
   Hark how the reeds are rustling.

From out its sheath he drew his heavy sword,
And clove the murderer's skull without a word.
Then bade the Bride go seek her lawful Lord
    Under the reeds high waving.

THE RING OF ST. MARK.

THE night was wild, the night was dark;
    And the little bark,
    By the quay of St. Mark,
Was rocking to burst its tether:
The boatman cowered, as the cold spray showered,
By Christ, 'twas an awful weather!

For three days the sea, against Venice driven,
Had no respite given,
Though the prayers to Heaven
Had in convent and church never ceased to sound;
The waters had risen in palace and prison,
And many in chains had been drowned.

The boatman suddenly 'came aware
That a figure was there
On the landing stair;
And a voice he heard in the gloom:
"Ferry me o'er, with a rapid oar
To St. George's island and tomb."

"With such waves as those? On such night as this?
When the wild winds hiss?
And the oar must miss
Every second stroke? Art mad?"
But the stranger said: "Neither doubt nor dread,
But row me across and be glad."

And the boatman, he knew not why, obeyed,
And ne'er felt afraid;
But a prayer he prayed,
While the gulls in the darkness screeched;
O'er the oars he bowed, through the waves he ploughed,
Till St. George's island was reached.

And the stranger said in a tone of command,
As he stepped on the sand
Of the island-strand:
"Await me, not long shall I be."
And the boatman discerned, when the stranger returned,
That a stately companion had he.

And a vivid flash showed a youthful knight
Clad in armour bright,
In a rosy light;
And he noted his beauty with wonder,

But the darkness came back, with the rattling crack
Of the strong and impatient thunder.

And the strangers said, "With thy stalwart oar
Do thou take us o'er
To the Lido's shore,
Where St. Nicholas lies in his tomb;
For the waters they menace the children of Venice
With a sudden and terrible doom."

And the boatman cried as his heart did fail,
"In this howling gale?
With this boat so frail?
It were death to make but the attempt!"
But the twain spake thus: "Put thy faith in us,
And from death we shall keep thee exempt."

And the boatman obeyed, he scarce knew why,
Though the waves whipped high,
And he feared to die;
And he felt they were drifting fast,
While the waves that were seething allowed him
    no breathing,
But they got to the Lido at last.

There the strangers said, in a tone of command
As they touched the sand

Of the longed-for strand;
"Await us, not long shall we be;"
And the boatman discerned when anon they re-
  returned,
That his passengers now were three.

For the boatman saw by a flash of white
And quivering light,
Which dispelled the night,
A figure unnoticed before;
On his head was a mitre; his beard it was whiter
Than the silvery stole he wore.

Then the strangers said: "Neither dread nor doubt,
But all danger scout;
Thou must row us out
To the broad, broad sea in thy boat."
But he cried all aghast, "In this horrible blast
Which knocketh the teeth down one's throat?"

Yet he knew not why, he obeyed again,
And with toil and pain
Sought the open main,
While fear did his face disfigure;
In the dark as they drifted, they felt themselves
  lifted
By waves that grew bigger and bigger.

Like a desperate man o'er his oars he bowed,
Through the dark he ploughed
While he prayed aloud,
And on Jesus and Mary did call;
While each flash that was vivid showed waves that
    were livid,
About to engulf them all.

And he suddenly saw, as his oar did dip,
In a hugh wave's tip,
What looked like a ship,
Whose sides were of sullen fire;
While devils in crowds were aloft in the shrouds
And the rigging of red-hot wire.

And the boatman saw, as he quaked with fear,
The strange ship veer,
And against them steer,
While the devils did jibber and taunt;
But his passengers three met the fiends of the sea,
And imperiously bade them avaunt.

"By the great God Christ, whom the Jews denied,
Who on Golgotha died,
To a cross-tree tied,
Why raise ye the waters thus?

Why make ye them menace the people of Venice,
Who fasten their faith on *us?*"

As the holy words from the speakers fell,
There was heard a yell,
Like the voice of Hell,
From the ship which the dark air rent;
Then she suddenly lurched with the fiends that
    were perched
In her rigging, and down she went.

Then a sudden lull. To the slimy caves,
Which be sailors' graves,
Retreated the waves,
While the whirlwind released fled home;
And the bright white moon peeped out right soon,
At the waters still covered with foam.

And the first of the three to the boatman said:
"Now the peril is fled,
And the Devils are dead,
And Venice no more need fear.
He who took thy bark was her own St. Mark,
With St. George and St. Nicholas here.

And lest any perchance should the danger scout,
Or the miracle doubt

Which thou givest out;
Go, take to the Doge this ring,
And bid Venice rejoice with thundering voice,
And praises eternally sing."

And the boatman did as the strangers taught,
And the Palace he sought,
And the ring he brought
To the Doge, all in state enthroned;
'Twas St. Mark's own ring, that most precious thing,
Which Venice for ages had owned.

THE EMPEROR ON THE LEDGE.

ABOUT A.D. 1500.

 A FEARFUL fall: a most prodigious fall!
Nay, wholly inconceivable!

                                    He rose,
Still clutching in his scraped and bleeding hands,
The weeds which he had snatched at as he fell;
And, dizzy still, looked up. From where he stood,
The maze of ledges and of pathless crags,
Down which by Heaven's guidance he had come,
Appeared a wall as smooth and as abrupt
As this last slope of rock down which he rolled,
And which forbade retreat, where stood he now?
He looked around: it was a narrow ledge,
Some ten yards long, which like a balcony,
Hung o'er he knew not what, for underneath
A sea of mist, with which the morning sun
Was just about to struggle, hid the view,
Adhering closely to the mountain's side.
So he must wait—Oh thrice unlucky chase!
Oh cursed impulse which had made him take,

The Emperor on the Ledge.

That shorter cut across the crags alone,
To mar a whole day's sport! 'Twas well indeed,
That he was gifted with a foot as sure,
A head as steady on the dizzy brink,
As any of his loyal Tyrolese,
Who trod these mountains; else the effigy
Upon the German ducats would have changed,
Before the time was ripe! a fearful fall,
A wondrous fall! but now the worst was o'er;
The lower ledges would be easier work,
And when this heavy mist had passed away,
He'd find a path.
              The mist dissolved.   He looked
And held his breath aghast: a precipice,
A thousand feet in depth, a wall of rock,
Unbroken by a single crack or ledge
Where bird might build, or weed might lodge its
    root,
Yawned sheer below him, till the grassy slopes,
Which met the strong and rapid Inn.   Beyond
Were fertile fields, with Innsbruck far away.

He sat him down to think; and well he might,
For in the prisons of his many lands
Was there a single captive whose escape
Seemed more impossible?   Help from below?
He crouched above the brink of the abyss

And tried to gauge its measureless extent
By the proportions of the things beneath;
And scanned the smoothness of the cruel rock,
Which was as vertical as is the shaft
Of a deep mine; and felt the answer,—No.
Help from above? Oh, who could find a path
Along the pathless sides of dizzy crags,
The labyrinths of ledges, he himself
Had crossed as by a miracle of God?
The prison chains which cramp and chafe the limbs,
The prison walls which slowly blunt the mind,
The prison bars which fret the pitying light,
Are full of horror and beget despair.
But this high dungeon open to the breeze,
Whose walls were space itself, whose vault was sky,
This narrow ledge, which seemed to say, " Remain
And die of thirst, and I will gently bleach
Thy unfound bones;" while cried the precipice—
" Leap; I will catch thee in my rocky lap,
" And men shall find thee and shall lay thee out
" In thy imperial robes." Oh, this was worse!

An hour had passed; the sun was rising high;
Beyond the river in the plain below
He saw the people working in the fields;
But far away, far out of reach of call;
O happy peasants, enviable boors,

The Emperor on the Ledge.

Free to depart, free to return at eve
To some rude hut, while he must perish here.
And though he knew that it was all in vain,
He shouted ever loudly into space,
Watching, the while, their hoes which rose and fell
With madening monotony; until,
By that strange weakness which awakens wrath
Against a man who hears not, he at length
Reviled them as base hounds, rebellious serfs,
Who let their Lord and Master vainly call,
And fiercely stamped his foot. They heard him not,
Nor turned in his direction, working on
As deaf and imperturbable as Fate.

An Emperor? an Emperor no more!
Thou art discrowned by Nature, not by Man,
She holds thee firmly in her mighty grip
And will not let thee go. Thy reign is o'er.
If thou wouldst still give orders and decrees,
Address them to the Elements; rebuke
The irksome wind; make treaties with the clouds,
Send forth the birds as thy ambassadors,
For sooner will they hearken than will men.
Speak out, speak out! Let Heaven hear thy voice;
Say "I am Maximilian, whom for years
Fortune has loved to favour: I am he

Who has been chosen to exalt his race."
Say "From the Danube to the Northern Sea,
I am the Master; and these hills are mine."
And beg one drop of water for thy thirst!

For now it was the noon; the fiery sun
Poured full and pitilessly on the rock,
Whose white and naked flank with blinding glare,
Was heating like a furnace more and more;
And not a tree, and not a jutting stone
To give him refuge; not a patch of shade
In which to crouch! O that he were but small,
And like the peeping lizard that he scared,
Could vanish in the rock. And all the while,
As if in mockery of his raging thirst,
There was that ample river at his feet,
Rolling its useless volume in his sight
Unceasingly. A single narrow cloud,
In all the vast expanse of dazzling blue,
Was slowly sailing onwards to the sun.
O welcome cloud! O kind and friendly cloud,
Miss not the mark! Diverge not from the course,
But throw a patch of shadow on this rock,
And stop the burning arrows for a while;
Or melt in natural pity and distil
A dozen drops of rain to wet his lips
Before thou passest on! But all in vain;

"O hideous situation, monstrous plight!"
Page 69.

The Emperor on the Ledge.

The fatal and inexorable cloud
Passed just below the sun.

    More hours went by
And brought no help and counsel, brought no
  change,
Except the alternations of despair,
Which now was sullen, now was lashed to rage—
O hideous situation, monstrous plight!—
To die unshriven, die unreconciled,
With that strong God whom kings so much offend,
Upon this rocky death-bed all alone.
How long would death be coming? Many days?
And what a death! To be perchance attacked
By screeching eagles ere his life was fled,
And by a hundred meaner birds, for whom
No corpse will be imperial; overhead
The kites already circled round and round.
But no, it was too hideous; better far
To choose his time and leap from off the ledge
Into the other world; and once again
He crouched above the brink and peered below,
And in his fevered fancy saw himself
Disfigured at the bottom of the chasm.
But stop! but stop! what moving thing was that,
Now stopping, now advancing? was't a goat?
Ay, ay, a goat, and now another goat,

And yet another; now he counted five.
The goats implied a goat-herd; and he strained
In hopes of seeing him. Ah, there he was.
How small he looked! He gave a desperate shout,
Which made the rock re-echo, but in vain.
The other heard him not, nor raised his head.
How make him hear? There were some largish
    stones
Upon the ledge; he dropped one o'er the brink
And saw it reach the bottom and rebound,
And saw the goats all scamper, and the man
Start up and look and watch him, and run off,
And then return with others.

       He was seen!
He was alone no longer! he had friends;
And to his heart there rushed a flood of joy,
But only for a moment; for his hope
Ebbed back with cruel quickness as he looked
Once more around him, and compared his chance,
The rock above, the precipice below.
What had he done, or what success achieved,
Except to fill the valley, and secure
Spectators for his agony? See there:
The crowd was swelling fast, and could do nought.
If all the many millions that he ruled
Were down below their zeal were no avail.

No hope,—no hope. He stripped the golden braid
From off his cap, and, taking up a stone,
He bound his tablets to it, and he wrote:
"I am the Emperor. If I must die,
Bring me the Sacraments to the rock's foot."
And dropped it o'er the brink.
                              And yet, O God,
Was he so surely doomed? Did Fate exact
This monstrous death so surely? Could it be
That fortune had befriended him through life
Only to bring him to this frightful end?
Was courage helpless? Could no human foot
Repeat the passage which had brought him here?
No daring soul, to save an Emperor,
Find, once again, that faint and dizzy path
From ledge to ledge and reach the cliff above,
And lower him a rope? Among the crowd
Assembled down below were fearless men,
Old hunters of the chamois, great of heart,
Who would, he knew, dispute his life with Heaven.
Was he not here among his Tyrolese,
Who loved him as a father? Would they let
Their Maximilian die? It must be long
Since he had thrown the tablets, for the crowd
Was now immense. The sun was getting low,
But still was there; the daylight would suffice;
And all to-morrow, yea and many days,

He could withstand the hunger and the thirst,
And burning heat, if only he were sure
That he had friends at work. But what was that?
There seemed a stir among the crowd below.
What lights were those which slowly wound along
Like tapers borne by priests? What sound was that
Which faintly reached him like a chant of monks?
He saw the people bare their heads and kneel
As through their midst a slow procession past
And halted at the bottom of the rock.
It was the Host.

      He bowed his head to Fate,
And, kneeling on the ledge, he stretched his hands
Towards the holy symbol down below,
Which could approach no nearer. Out beyond
The sun was setting with a wondrous glow
Of such translucent colours as may shine
On angels' wings. The whole horizon seemed
Converted into glory, and the clouds,
Which streaked the sea of amber, seemed the steps
Of the Eternal Throne. He gazed awhile,
And felt his anguish mingling with the skies
In infinite solemnity and peace,
He faintly murmured, "I accept Thy will,"
And would have risen when he felt a hand
Laid gently on his shoulder. He was saved.

THE KEYS OF THE CONVENT.

PART I.

THE night had closed, and all reposed
    Within the Convent's walls,
The cloisters fair now empty were,
    And silent were the halls.

And undisturbed, with passions curbed
    The Nuns to rest had gone;
The moonbeams peeping could see them sleeping,
    Each in her cell of stone.

But there was one, the portress nun,
    Whom mighty struggles tried;
With breathing bated, awake she waited
    A well-known step outside.

She crouched with shame, where burnt the flame
    Before the Virgin's figure;
And, as she knelt, each moment felt
    Her bursting heart grow bigger.

"O Mary mild, and Holy Child,"
   She cried with burning brow,
"Oh give me power, this bitter hour,
   To keep my convent vow;

"See how I fight, this live-long night
   With fierce temptation near;
When Love shall call, prevent my fall,
   Vouchsafe my prayer to hear."

And at the feet of Mary sweet
   The sister portress lay
Convulsed and pale, with groan and wail,
   Nor ceased for help to pray.

But soon outside was heard a stride
   Distinctly more and more,
And there was heard a whispered word,
   Athrough the grated door:

"Away, away, 'tis almost day,
   My steed hard by is waiting;
I cannot wait; 'tis late, 'tis late,
   Unfasten quick the grating."

She gave a start, loud thumped her heart
   And to her feet she leapt;

By passion urged, by conscience scourged,
    Half to the door she stept.

There, all unnerved, she now observed
    The door, and now the shrine,
Where fair and mild, the Virgin smiled
    Her smile of love Divine.

"Once gone with *him*, oh who will trim
    Thy lamp that's ever burning,
Or wreathe thy flowers in noon-tide hours,
    When once there's no returning?"

"I've not the strength," she gasped at length,
    "I've not the strength to stay;"
As more and more outside the door,
    Was heard the call "Away!"

But ere she fled, with muffled head,
    She kissed the Virgin's knees,
And in her charge, she left the large
    And heavy Convent keys.

II.

She drank her measure of sinful pleasure;
    At last the dregs were met,
The more they thickened the more she sickened,
    But thicker grew they yet.

She looked around; no help she found,
   She dared not look above;
She could no more to Heaven soar
   Than a bespattered dove.

But from her life with scandal rife,
   She now with loathing turned,
And for the end, which God should send,
   From dawn to eve she yearned.

At last one day she tore away
   The jewelled chain she wore;
The silken dress which did oppress,
   From off her limbs she tore;

And donned again her old and plain
   And cherished Nun's attire
Hid in her trunk, and which she'd shrunk
   From giving to the fire.

And courage rallied and firmly sallied
   When Day was nearly spent;
On, on, she flew, though well she knew
   What was the punishment.

She sighted late the Convent gate,
   Sound slept the pious flock;

The Keys of the Convent.

And lo, the door revolved before
   Her hand had time to knock.

What could it mean? Had she been seen?
   She shyly stepped within,
No soul was there? The Portress where?
   And who had let her in?

But in the shrine, the lamp did shine
   Before the Virgin's figure,
In whose white hand the keys did stand.
   Her awe grew ever bigger.

She knelt again in fear and pain,
   As on that fatal night,
And the Mother of God appeared to nod
   By the uncertain light.

And there she stay'd, and humbly prayed
   Until the matins rang,
Then, pale of face, she took her place
   Among the nuns who sang.

But in their eyes was no surprise,
   As if they'd never missed her;
None seemed amazed; no cry was raised,
   That 'twas their erring sister.

She asked of one: Which was the nun
    Who now was Portress there?
But, stranger yet, her words were met
    By Wonder's gaping stare.

Ye Saints above! Her sinful love,
    Had it been nought but dreaming?
And was her flight that fatal night,
    And her return, mere seeming?

"But no, but no," she murmured low,
    "Her sin was but too real,"
When a sudden thought at which she caught,
    Brought light in her ordeal.

When she had fled with muffled head,
    While all in peace did sleep,
Had she not given the Queen of Heaven
    The Convent keys to keep?

And could it be, that even she
    Had done the sinner's duty,
And service done to save the nun
    Betrayed by Youth and Beauty.

She knelt again, but not in pain;
    Oh, had she guessed aright?
And the mother of God, appeared to nod
    In the uncertain light.

THE BELL FOUNDER OF AUGSBURG.

 MIGHTY bell that's slowly tolling,
With a deep and mellow boom,
High above the life that's rolling
From the cradle to the tomb;
A mighty bell, which those of old
Have heard, and which shall still be tolled
For generations yet unborn;
A mighty bell whose brazen voice
Now bids the City to rejoice,
And now with all its heart to mourn;
A mighty bell which lives the life
Of the people, and recordeth
Fire, and Flood, and City-strife,
And whate'er the Lord awardeth
That the pregnant years should bring,
Is a grand and solemn thing.

And of such a bell as this,
Tolling o'er the deep abyss,
From its great Cathedral Tower

In the dusky twilight hour;
Filling with its measured boom
All the gloom;
Let me now the story tell.
How the earliest note that sounded
From the giant newly founded
Was its maker's passing knell.

For this is what the legend says:
At Augsburg in the olden days,
Before King Weather seized his palette
And painted grey the City's towers
With winter storms and summer showers
Before King Time took up his mallet
And left his dints and cruel traces,
On the fair fronts of holy places;
At Augsburg—when throughout the land
Rose many a minster rich and grand,
When towered cites, strong and free,
Whose narrow gabled streets were filled
With waving flags of many a guild,
Were homes of proud activity;
When goldsmiths wrought with patient chisel,
A lifetime ere a chain was made,
And armourers with age would grizzle
While stooping o'er a single blade—
There lived a very famous founder

The Bell Founder of Augsburg.

Of bells, whose name was Master John.
No founder cast a metal sounder,
Or bells more fair to look upon;
His great big bells, all sunny yellow,
Gave out a sound superb and mellow;
In all that country he alone
Could give the true, the glorious tone,
And knew the secret of the proper
Proportion of the tin and copper;
And whereso'er a Gothic spire
At last had ceased to rise still higher,
The priests who sought sonorous bronze
Were sure to go to Master John's.

He was a strong and earnest man,
Of aspect rough, and over fifty;
Self-made and sober, ever thrifty,
Whose beard to grizzle had begun;
A man unswerving, and whose heart
Was wholly given to his art:
A man of work, a man of will,
A man of thought and patient skill;
Upon whose bronzed and furrowed brow
The sweat but seldom ceased to flow;
A man to all the town endeared,
And whom alone the idle feared,
For all his 'prentices agreed

That if his wrath was rashly vented,
His heart was kind, and he repented
As quickly of the word or deed.
A many were the bells he founded,
And all had to his fame redounded;
And not a few were big, I ween;
And yet his mind ne'er ceased to dwell
Upon a bigger, mightier bell
Than any he had made or seen.
But how and when? No bell was needed
Of such a size. The years succeeded
Each other, and no order came;
But yet he planned it all the same,
And firmly cherished the persuasion
That God would send him the occasion.
And so indeed the thing befell.
One day the city's largest bell,
Which hands, long turned to dust, had cast,
With toil and trouble in the past,
Uttered its last vibrating cry,
(For bells, like men, at length must die),
And it was settled by the people
That in the great and empty steeple
A greater, mightier, bell should stand,
Louder than any in the land;
A bell, whose every echoing note
Should o'er the town and suburbs float.

He framed the giant model slowly,
For loving work abhorreth haste;
And every scroll and garland wholly
With his own hand the master traced.
He gave it with a secret joy
A curve unknown to bells in use;
And planned a new and bold alloy
Which should a wondrous tone produce.
No labour and no pain he shirked;
But oft alone at night he worked,
Moulding the city's old escutcheon,
Until the morning stars were dim,
Or slowly carving the inscription,
Which ran in couplets round the rim:—

>   Sleep secure; for I will call
>   If the foe approach the wall.

>   Sleep secure; for from my spire
>   I will raise the cry of fire.

>   Sleep secure; for I will wake you
>   Ere the swollen stream o'ertake you.

>   Where I toll may corn and wine
>   Never fail, nor fatten'd kine.

The Bell Founder of Augsburg.

    Where I toll may men agree,
    Living orderly and free.

    Where I toll may justice reign
    In the city and the plain.

And so the Master worked away,
He and his men for many a day;
Until the well-baked mould of clay,
Wall'd deep within the ground, and steady
As Earth itself, at last was ready;
And till the furnace loud was roaring,
And all was over, save the pouring.

'Twas late at night. The mingled metals
Were letting wholesome bubbles rise;
And God, who every issue settles,
Appeared to bless the enterprise.
But Master John, whose practised glance
Observed the glowing surface dance
With transient gleams of lurid red,
Knew well that time must still elapse,
Unless he wished to court mishaps;
And to his 'prentices he said:
"Now will I leave you for a little;
The bell, cast now, would be but brittle;
Ye all have eaten and have rested

At various times throughout the day;
But I nor food nor rest have tasted,
Since early morn was cold and gray."
And then he bade the 'prentice Fritz,
His chosen lad of ready wits,
To watch with care the molten ore,
While he himself should step next door
To snatch a meal, and quaff a clear
And foaming mug of nut-brown beer.

The 'prentice Fritz, when he was gone,
Sat by the molten mass alone;
And watched the metal surface shiver,
With lurid eddies circling ever.
Some say that evil spirits lurk
In molten ore and mischief work,
Bewitching luckless wights who look
Too long at metals as they cook,
And leading wretches on at times
To fatal ills or mighty crimes.
Did some such spirit now decoy,
The lad who watched the new alloy?
I know not: but he seemed to hear
Strange whispered words, nor far nor near.
The metal said, Oh let me flow
At once into the mould below;
Why make me on this furnace linger,

When thou need'st only raise a finger?
Why make me wait another hour,
Oh thou that hast me in thy power?
And as the 'prentice looked and listened,
And saw the bronze that seethed and glistened;
His fingers itched to touch the sluice,
And let the restless monster loose.
With guilty eyes he round him glanced;
His hand advanced, withdrew, advanced;
Till, all at once the fiery-hot
And hissing metal forward shot,
And while the smoke in volumes rolled,
All prematurely filled the mould.

Scarce was the senseless act committed
Than sense with crushing weight returned;
And all the measure of his folly
The luckless Fritz with fear discerned.
The mould, constructed at such cost,
Was doubtless split; the bell was lost,
The work of months, the dream of years,
The object of all hopes and fears.
The mighty bell, which Master John
Had lavished all his skill upon,
Was now no more, but would be found
Mere shapeless rubbish in the ground.
With guilty fear the 'prentice trembled,

Yet all his courage he assembled,
And had sufficient strength to run
And stammer out what he had done.
The rough and grizzly John was seated
Over his meal, his knife in hand.
He stared, nor seemed to understand;
But when he heard the words repeated,
The blood rushed fiercely to his head;
A sudden flush his face o'erspread.
And cursing, at a single bound
He fell upon him like a hound,
And with his knife he struck him dead.

An awful stillness follows sudden crimes.
The furious wave, which has o'erwhelmed and swallowed
Our innocence, by sudden calm is followed,
As are the squalls of tempest-troubled climes.
No outward stir betrays the wreck beneath;
The wave has passed, and underneath is death.
The wretch, in dull dejection, scarcely knows
Why all is changed, or how the storm arose.
No tempest yesterday, and none to-day;
But, 'tween the two, a fatal minute lies,
And if to-day is calm, no sunbeams play
Upon the waves, and leaden are the skies.

As Master John in prison lay,
And weeks passed emptily away,
Was it the 'prentice or the bell
He brooded over,—who can tell?
Perchance it was o'er both; they blended
In one dull, aching sense of loss,
Of ruined life, of honour ended,
As on his mattress he would toss.
In silent apathetic gloom,
He heard himself condemned to death:
What need, he thought, of life's sweet breath
To one on whom there is a doom?
For he had loved the lad he killed;
And when he thought how brave, and skilled,
And young he was, an anguish filled
His soul; he cursed the deed he'd done,
And felt as if he'd slain a son.
And then, again, his thoughts would dwell
There, in his narrow prison cell,
Upon his great and ill-starred bell.
Until at night, when dreams have power,
He fancied for a transient hour
That nought had happened, nought was wrong;
And that the bell, superb and strong,
Amid the shouting of the throng,
Was being hoisted to its tower,

Where with its big and brazen voice
It cried to all: Rejoice, Rejoice!

There was a custom, born of pity,
And immemorial, in the city:
That in each Year of Jubilee,
A death-doomed captive, not o'erhardened,
Should by the magistrates be pardoned,
And straightway set at liberty.
The city's rulers sent to fetch,
Four times each century, some wretch
On whom the sun had hopeless risen,
And bade him, ere he left his prison,
Give thanks to God, for he was free.
Now this same year just chanced to be
The holy Year of Jubilee;
And Master John, as all expected,
Was for this special grace selected.
But when they came he shook his head:
"It cannot be," he simply said,
"And all your arguments are vain.
The blow is struck, the lad is dead,
And nought can give him life again.
Upon the big and luckless bell,
On whose account all this befel,
I wrote, and now would write again:
Where I shall toll let Justice reign."

If ye, who judged me, have forgiven,
So have not I, nor yet hath Heaven;
Then let me die, and grant his life
To some poor wretch who hath a wife
And children; I, ye know, have none."

So spake he, and the thing was done.
Upon the morrow, ere the sun
Had risen, and the birds begun
To twitter and each other waken;
From out his prison he was taken
Towards the execution place.
It was a square and ample space,
Already filled for many an hour;
Beyond it loomed a dusky tower,
Above the roofs immensely high,
Against the morning's crimson sky.
It was the same in which his bell,
Had it not perished, now would dwell;
And heeding not the seething throng
He fixed his eyes upon it long,
As if its form possessed a spell.
But suddenly the prisoner started,
His pallid lips in rapture parted;
For from the tower in the gloom
There came a great and mellow boom
As of a bell, and then a second.

He knew it well: it was his own:
His own great bell, which could alone
Give out that deep and glorious tone:
That wondrous sound on which he'd reckoned,
When in his shop with secret joy
He first had planned his new alloy;
So, after all, that bell so cherished,
So mourned, so fatal, had not perished!
With steady step and radiant face
He climbed the steps and took his place,
And in the tolling read that Heaven,
Approved his death, and had forgiven.

THE WITNESS.

THE rising sun, the setting sun, was Spanish.
It was the time when Spain at length had clutched
Those phantom islands which would loom and vanish,
  Where western skies the western billows touched.
It was the time when Spain's o'er restless souls
Were made the lords of undiscovered realms;
And Spanish ships that boldly turned their helms,
Towards Fancy's ports and Dreamland's airy goals,
Would reach instead some strange substantial shore.
It was the time when old and wrinkled creatures,
Seeking in Florida the fount of youth,
Would taste each spring, and then survey their features
Reflected in its surface, where the truth
Too harshly told, but made them search the more ;
It was the time when every hungry scholar,

With gaping elbows and with ragged collar,
Might dream of foot-prints left in sands of gold,
And Indian streams whose waters rubies rolled;
Of monstrous gems in Aztec temples stored;
And sell his books to buy himself a sword.

Just such a scholar, full of restless dreams,
Dwelt in a city where the Tagus streams;
Which city I forget; it little matters:
It had grandees, and crowds in rags and tatters;
And tattered was young Blas, although in truth
Nature had shaped him for a handsome youth;
And had his body been less gaunt and lean,
And his apparel less unstitched and mean,
He might have hoped to captivate a queen.
As matters stood, he had transfixed the heart
Of no one save a sempstress; but the dart
Had firmly lodged, for in Teresa's eyes
There was no leanness in him—only beauty.

She was a patient girl, who loved to rise
At break of day and shirked no irksome duty.
Her dearest wish—the day-dream of her life—
Was to become this shabby scholar's wife.
She long had hoped, with their united earnings,
To reach this end, the goal of all her yearnings,
And laboured hard with courage and with skill

To save a little; work was paid but ill.
But not a rap the hungry scholar earned,
And oft she lent him what he ne'er returned.
He loathed his books, he loathed his three-legged
    stool,
And thought each learned teacher but a fool.
What, work all day, to be a lawyer's drudge,
And dull and fameless to an office trudge;
When valiant captains on the coast unfurled
Their daring banners for the new-found world!
What, drive a quill, and copy by the hour,
When rapid paths led on to fame and power!
Not he, not he. And so one day he told
Teresa he was leaving, and had sold
His books to buy an outfit, and would leave
To seek his fortune o'er the western seas;
That he would soon return; she must not grieve,
But bow her head to Heaven's wise decrees.
Why should she sob and wildly wring her hands,
For her alone he sought those distant lands.
He would return enriched, no longer needy
As now he was—the road to wealth was speedy—
And then they should get married, for he knew
That she would wait with patience and be true.

It chanced that, when he told her, they were walking
In the old gothic cloisters, where their talking

"Nay, even by this crucifix I swear it,
And from my heart I call on Christ to hear it."

Page 95.

The Witness.

Had no observers. 'Twas a fair retreat
Where hollow echoes from beneath their feet
Revealed the dwellings of eternal sleepers;
While through the gothic lace-work might be seen
The waving leaves, and tendrils fresh and green,
Of o'er-luxuriant and intrusive creepers.
The scholar and the maiden were alone;
The only thing which human shape possessed
Was the Redeemer's figure, looking down
With half closed lids, as if by pain oppressed,
From a great Cross. And, as the couple passed
Before this Cross, the scholar stopped, and said,
While on the holy form a look he cast:
"I will return and thee alone will wed,
Nay, even by this crucifix I swear it,
And from my heart I call on Christ to hear it."

And so young Blas, the hungry scholar, started
Upon his journey, all the more light-hearted
That in his knapsack lay Teresa's savings.
When he set off it was the close of day,
The setting sun appeared to point the way
To those far shores, the object of his cravings;
But for Teresa, as she lingered still,
When he was out of sight upon the hill,
The evening's many shadows seemed to fall
Upon her heart like a funeral pall.

Through distant mists, its fatal journey done,
Large, round, and rayless, slowly sank the sun.
It touched the plain; she watched its lobe diminish,
As if all gladness with its sight must finish.
For some few moments, after it had dipt,
Each passing cloud with crimson light was tipt;
Then all was grey, and distant sounds which fell
Upon her ear were like a faint farewell.

Then one by one the tardy years went by,
Each like the last, nor brought they his returning.
The sempstress sat and sewed, and, with a sigh,
Counted the days in undiminished yearning.
Years eight; years nine; years ten, and still she waited,
Nor ceased to think that his return was fated.
She questioned many soldiers from Peru
And Mexico, but none her lover knew.
They told her of the dangers men must run
Who sought the countries of the setting sun;
How sudden fever made them lose their hold
Of long-sought gems and hardly-gotten gold;
How Indian slaves rose up against their lords,
Inventing deaths unpaintable by words;
How Christian soldiers turned upon each other,
And, for a bauble, brother murdered brother.

She shuddered as she listened, but she never
Allowed these tales the thread of hope to sever.

One day a soldier whom she thus had questioned
Told her a famous captain would arrive
Soon in that city, by whose good assistance
It might be learnt if Blas was still alive;
A man of note in Transatlantic lands,
Who knew the leaders of all Spanish bands,
The very man to help her; when he came
Let her apply, Rodriguez was his name.

The great man came, she waited near his inn
With beating heart, as if it were a sin;
At last he sallied forth: his martial look,
His sword which clicked at every step he took,
His cloak of scarlet thrown across his shoulder,
Were little fit to make the suitor bolder;
But scarcely did her eyes his features scan,
Than with a shriek she wildly forward ran
And clutched his arm, for in that warlike man
She recogised her Blas. But with a wrench
He freed his arm—" What means," he cried, " this wench,
What mean her words? I swear I know her not,"
And from his eyes a look of menace shot.
" Blas, Blas," she cried in tones that cruelly faltered,

"Dost thou not know me? Am I wholly altered?"
But with a look that was more threat'ning still,
"Begone," he cried, "or it shall fare thee ill!
Leave me in peace, I know thee not, I say,"
And with an oath he bade her pass her way,
While she, down sinking, clasped his knees in
    vain,
And all bewildered struggled to detain.

A crowd had gathered, none in pity stared,
But at her cost nor gibe nor joke was spared;
Until Rodriguez, with a voice of thunder,
Ended the scene, and forced the throng asunder;
And she half senseless mid the ceaseless scoff,
Was roughly taken up, and carried off
To the Corregidor's.

                The stern old man,
Who held that weighty office in the city,
Was more renowned for justice than for pity;
And with a frown, to try the case began.
"Woman," he said, "a grave offence is thine,
Which will be punished both by jail and fine,
Unless thou canst adduce good exculpation;
For thou art charged with wanton molestation,
And public outrage to a Cavalier;
So make thy best defence; explain away

What thou hast done, or for his pardon pray
In true repentance, so that all may hear."

Teresa raised her head and eyed the judge,
And then the crowd, and then the judge again;
And with that eloquence which God doth grudge
To none, however lowly, when in pain,
She poured a flood of words, and not in vain,
For all were forced to listen, even he
Who had most reason to detest her plea;
"A devil, oh, a devil's in his heart,"
She fiercely cried, "that steals away his honour,
And makes him lie, and play a villain's part
To her he loved, and heap up outrage on her.
He sought my love, he bound himself by oath,
Then sailed for riches, riches for us both;
And now he knows me not, and swears to Heaven
He ne'er hath seen me, nor hath pledges given.
I care not for his wealth, I want his love;
Nay less, a kindly look. But doth he move?
I know I now am plain, ten years have passed
Since he went off, and beauty fadeth fast;
The more so as I stinted and lived scant,
Lest when he came he should be still in want.
I claimed no right. If only he had said
'I know thee well, and mind me of old times,
Thou art the woman that I swore to wed;

But I have prospered in those distant climes,
I now am rich and great, and thou art poor,'
I should have bowed my head and should have stood
Among the crowd of beggars at his door,
To see him pass; it would have done me good.
But to be cheated of a single nod,
To be denied the pittance of a smile,
To hear him say, and say again, O God,
That he ne'er saw my face, while all the while
I can read recognition in his eyes,
Which say distinctly what his tongue denies;
I've not the strength."

    The old Corregidor,
Whose rugged face a gentler aspect wore,
Reluctantly replied, "What can I say?
Thou hearest what he answers; That this day
He first beholds thy face; that thou art mad,
Or that from secret motives, base and bad,
Thou hast against him lifted up thy voice.
Between his word and thine I have no choice,
Thou hast adduced no proof, nor called a witness;
There yet is time, therefore bethink thee well;
Hast thou no friend? none whom thou canst compel
To speak? For if thou hast one, in all fitness
He must be heard."

Teresa shook her head.
"Alas," she slowly and in sadness said,
"'Tis ten years back; and when this man did swear
One day to wed me, not a soul was there.
We were alone together, and the place
Was the old gothic cloister, lone and bare,
But wait, but wait"—and on the speaker's face
A strange and sudden inspiration shone,
"I have, I have, a witness! There is one
Who silently looked on, and must have heard
As we were talking, every single word!
You all must know the lofty cross which stands
Against the wall, where Christ with punctured hands
Hangs long, and lean and livid, looking down,
With blood drops trickling from his thorny crown;
Go seek this Christ, and take his deposition,
For something tells me that it will be given.
Go," she repeated with a wild decision,
"Go seek him quick, for I appeal to Heaven!"

A murmur of derision from the crowd, which filled the hall compactly,
Met at first her strange proposal, while the Captain burst
Into a laugh as angry as 'twas loud,
"Did I not say the woman's mad?" he cried,

"'Tis time, methinks, to let her hands be tied;"
But, with rebuking gesture of the hand,
The magistrate in tone of stern command
Bade all attend, and check unseemly mirth.
"There be," he said, "strange things upon this earth,
Neither too rashly laugh, nor rashly scout,
For there be cases when, beyond a doubt,
This Christian country's most religious laws
Allow the parties to transfer their cause
To better hands than man's, and to appeal
To miracle; not oft doth God reveal
The truth directly, but at times he doth,
And then it profits Faith and Morals both.
I therefore mean, without a moment's loss,
To send my scribe and guard of halberdiers
To crave this attestation from the Cross
In due and legal form. For it appears
(At least to my frail reason), most unfit,
That I, an earthly Judge, should judging sit
In presence of the effigy of Him
Who raised the Dead and on the waters trod,
And can throw light where all for man is dim;
With such a witness none may judge but God."

And so that summer evening, as the sun
To wane on the horizon had begun,
And in farewell dispatched a slanting ray

"The halberdiers
First having in a circle taken station
Around the Cross, the scribe (as it appears
From ancient records), made devout prostration."

Page 103.

To kiss the cloisters, and their columns gray;
An unaccustomed sound of trampling feet
Disturbed the silence of the lone retreat.
With rapid steps the motley small procession,
Which sought the place for Heaven's intercession,
Made straight for the great Crucifix, on which
A flood of colour, warm and soft and rich,
Direct descended, making strangely vivid
The dead Redeemer's limbs, which now not livid,
But full of life appeared.

    The halberdiers
First having in a circle taken station
Around the Cross, the scribe (as it appears
From ancient records), made devout prostration;
Then took his little ink-horn from his belt,
And with one knee upon the pavement knelt,
The while upon the other knee he rested
The legal form which was to be attested.
Upon his right the haughty captain stood
In sullen silence liking ill the jest;
While on his left, all muffled in her hood,
Teresa waited with a heaving breast.
"Jesus, the Son of God," the scribe began
"Who to redeem men's sins becameth human,
Dost Thou bear solemn witness that this man
Did in Thy presence swear to wed this woman?"

There was a pause; all present fixed their eyes
Upon the Cross in breathless mute surmise,
Even the doubters in their very doubt.
And well they might, for wonder's sudden shout
From every mouth a mighty portent hailed—
The carved Redeemer suddenly unnailed
 His arm from off the wood, and stretched it out
Like one who takes an oath; while some declared
That through his lifeless lips there passed a " Yes."

Upon the word I lay but little stress,
But this is certain that this selfsame Christ
Can still be seen by any that may care:
The arm is stretched as in the act of giving
An attestation; less has oft sufficed
In pious lands to keep a legend living.

THE RIDE OF DON PEDRO.

DON PEDRO was riding his horse at a walk,
    Through the streets of an old Spanish city;
When, a little ahead, he perceived that there sped
    A figure uncommonly pretty.

The lady appeared in a hurry to be,
    For she looked not behind her nor tarried;
Nor too short, nor too tall, while her ankle was small,
    And her veil she bewitchingly carried.

Now it chanced that, like many a brave cavalier,
    For small ankles the Don had a weakness;
So he woke up his steed which was moving indeed
    At a leisurely pace in its sleekness.

But, though long was the stride of the beautiful bay,
    He stepped not as fast as the lady,

With her sweet little feet she took street after street,
  Through the gates to an alley all shady.

Don Pedro then touched up his steed with his spur;
  He trotted, but great was his wonder,
For fast though his trot he caught her up not:
  Twelve yards ever kept them asunder!

He cantered; he galloped; O prodigy strange,
  In spite of the horse's endeavour,
And hard though he whipped, ahead she still tripped,
  No nearer he got to her ever.

No further, no nearer, she seemed than before,
  Though the bounds of his horse were gigantic;
Over hill, over dale, with the speed of the gale,
  He followed her ever more frantic.

Through cornfield and meadow, and forest and moor;
  Over furrow, and heather, and shingle,
Over dale, over hill, she was luring him still,
  When sunlight and starlight did mingle.

Past flew the villages, past flew the towns,
  The cornfields no more did he ravage;

But through marshes he dashes where the water
    high splashes,
  The country was lone and was savage.

"I'll reach her! I'll catch her!" he shouted with
    rage,
  "Though I ride to the end of creation!"
As he tore through the loam, from his horse flew
    the foam,
  And he spurred with a wild desperation.

He thought he was gaining upon her at last;
  "I've caught her, I've caught her!" he shouted;
And he goaded his horse with his uttermost force
  Till the blood from his nostrils was spouted.

"I hold her!" he shouted, as wildly he dashed
  Through the waterless bed of a river;
But his horse sudden sank, on his spur-reddened
    flank,
  And died with a groan and a quiver.

Then only, the lady stopped short and turned round;
  And the form he had thought to admire,
So graceful of limb, stood terrific and grim,
  A skeleton filled with fire.

THE IMPIOUS STONE.

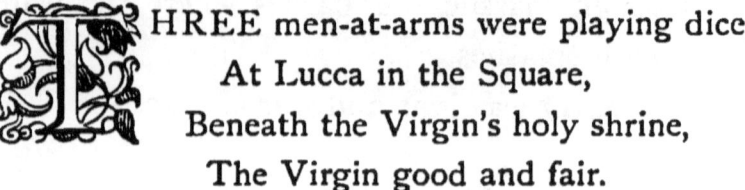HREE men-at-arms were playing dice,
    At Lucca in the Square,
Beneath the Virgin's holy shrine,
    The Virgin good and fair.

An image painted in the past,
    Of aspect sweet and mild,
Sustaining, on her rounded arm,
    The halo-crownéd Child.

One of the players lost his stake,
    And lost again, and thrice;
And, with a loud and impious oath,
    He cursed the rattling dice.

And on the bench, with heavy fist,
    An angry blow he struck;
"It is that Virgin there," he cried,
    "That brings me this ill luck!"

The Impious Stone.

Again the rattling dice he raised,
   And on the bench he tossed:
It was his last remaining coin,
   And once again he lost.

Then, in his rage, he seized a stone
   And hurled it at the shrine;
And would, so well the stone was aimed,
   Have hit the Child divine.

When, O miraculous event!
   O rare and wondrous sight!
The Virgin shifted, quick as thought,
   The Child from left to right.

The stone the Virgin's shoulder struck,
   Just where the Babe had stood,
And from the painted shoulder flowed,
   In trickling rills, the blood.

The men-at-arms, with gaping face,
   Beheld the shoulder bleed;
Then turned to him who in his wrath
   Had done the impious deed.

But what was not their quake and dread,
   When they perceived that he

Into the pavement of the square,
   Was rooted like a tree!

In vain he writhed, in vain he tugged;
   In vain the air he beat;
In vain he swore blaspheming oaths,
   The pavement locked his feet.

"Atone! Atone!" his comrades cried,
   "The Virgin's peace implore!"
But at the shrine he shook his fist,
   And only cursed the more.

Then sank he to his waist in earth.
   He fiercely ground his teeth;
In vain he tugged, in vain he writhed;
   Hell sucked him from beneath.

"Atone!" his comrades cried again,
   And make thy peace with Heaven;
Atone, atone! There still is time,
   Thou still may'st be forgiven!"

But with a yet more hideous oath,
   Again he shouted, "No!
I'll not retract, I'll not atone,
   Although to Hell I go!"

"Then sank he to his waist in earth.
He fiercely ground his teeth;
In vain he tugged, in vain he writhed;
Hell sucked him from beneath."

Above his shoulders then he sank;
   His head alone remained,
A horrid and malignant head,
   With eyes that rolled and strained.

And soon it disappeared as well;
   The man-at-arms was gone,
Who at the Virgin's holy shrine,
   Had thrown the impious stone.

A RIVAL OF FALLOPIUS.

"Princeps jubet ut nobis dent hominem, quem nostro modo interficimus et illum anatomisamus."—*Fallopius*, A.D. 1550.

E was undoubtedly awake; but where?—
As consciousness had gradually returned,
It had, at first, assumed the shape of dreams.
It seemed to him that in a block of ice,
His body was fast locked; and that in vain
He tried to move his limbs, while chill on chill
Ran through his very marrow. Then anon
It seemed to be a coffin dark and cold,
In which he was enclosed deep underground.
And yet how could it be? His arms were stretched
Like Christ's upon the cross. *Was* it a cross
To which he fast was nailed—a cross laid flat;
For certainly he lay upon his back;
And now was most undoubtedly awake.
He felt his eyelids open in the dark.
He gave a shout, and to his shout there came,
A sort of moan in answer, like the whine

Of some dumb dying animal; and then
There rose a chorus of short wheezing yelps,
Unutterably frightful and grotesque.
Where could he be?

     He tried to fix his thoughts;
And recollect what things he last had seen,
And where he last had stood. Where had it been?
Ah, now he had it!—Yes; he saw himself,
Carelessly, idle, sitting on the wall,
Watching the lizards in the evening sun,
Peeping from holes and darting at the flies;
And, as he so was sitting, there had passed
Along the street a sickly looking man,
Robed like a man of medicine or of law;
Who, stopping, with a nod had said, " My lad,
I see thee daily sitting on this wall:
Hast thou no work or calling? What's thy name?'
That he had answered that his name was John,
That, as for work he cared not much for that,
But loved the sun and nutting in the woods;
That he oft earned a trifle by odd jobs,
Or running errands: and that then the man
Had said, " I have a job for thee to do,
I will return and fetch thee after dark.
Which he had done, and led him to a house,
Where he had given him to eat and drink,

That then he had felt drowsy; this was all
He could remember. Oh how cold he felt,
How cold and stiff! Again he tried to move,
To burst the unseen bonds which held him down.
He wore himself with shouting; all in vain,
No answer came, save that strange wheezing sound.

By slow degrees he then became aware
Of something like a whiteness overhead
Which faintly grew and seemed to be the light,
The light of morning such as it descends
Through cellar windows; and from out the gloom
Surrounding things emerged. What first he saw
Was his own body, white and wholly stripped,
Strapped down upon a table. Then the light,
In creeping slowly onward to the left,
Showed him another form still indistinct,
Upon the selfsame table. Like himself,
It lay upon its back and seemed strapped down ;
The head alone moved ever and anon
From side to side. 'Twas smaller than a man ;
It surely was a woman or a child,
But all deformed and like those goblin shapes
Which jutted from the old cathedral's sides.
He strained to see the features; very strange
The shape they took: How long appeared the face!
The light increased; he saw it was a dog.

A Rival of Fallopius.

From underneath its back a thin red rill
Was slowly trickling o'er the table's edge,
Where lay strange knives and tweezers and—
    O God—
He saw no more, could look no more, a weight
Of horror closed his eyes, until a sound,
As of a gently opening door, disturbed
The silence of the place; he raised his lids.
There stood that same bent, sickly-looking man,
With high bald forehead and with thin white lips.
A boundless joy o'erfilled the captive's heart.
"Quick, quick," he cried, "Untie, untie me quick!
Oh, quick unstrap the thong! Who tied me down?
What place is this?"

                            But strange to say,
The other answered not, nor nearer came;
But, going to a drawer some paces off,
Began to rummage slowly in its depths;
And though the captive never ceased to call,
Seemed not to heed him; only once he paused,
And fixed upon him one long vacant look
Such as we fix on some inanimate thing
When lost in thought—O Christ, what could it
    mean?
Why did he stand and rummage in the drawer
And not untie him? he who over night

Had been so kind and friendly. And the joy,
The hope of prompt release, began to change
Into a weird and undefinable fear.
And when he saw him close the drawer at last,
And silently approach, he straightway shrank,
He knew not why; a thin white hand was laid
Upon the thong; but 'twas to readjust,
To tighten, not to free. The captive saw,
And understood the action, for he gave
A sort of wail, and cried "What have I done?
What do you want? What is this dreadful place?
Oh, let me go; I am an orphan lad
Who lives from hand to mouth, and does no harm.
Is this a torture room? Oh, I will speak,
But do not hurt me,—I will answer all,
I will reveal, I will reveal."

        The man
Who until now had seemed absorbed in thought;
Mute and as unattentive to his words
As to the fitful moaning of the dog,
Upon his human captive fixed his eyes,
Where flashed a sudden fervour, and exclaimed
Half to himself: "Reveal? ay, that thou shalt.
Thou shalt reveal inestimable truths
Of which thou knowest nothing; thou shalt tell
Secrets unknown to men, but guessed by me;
Thou shalt confirm what these dumb dogs have told

Beneath the scalpel; thou shalt be the last
And chiefest witness;" and he laid his hand
Upon the heap of little shining knives
Which lay upon the table.

                      Strange and vague
As were his words, the victim understood
Their terrible significance; they meant
The imminence of torture; for he burst
Into a loud and deafening appeal
For help, for mercy, for delay; he yelled
For God, for men; he shouted and he sobbed;
He prayed, he threatened, offered to reveal
He knew not what, betray he knew not whom.
God answered not.

                The man seemed not to hear
The ever louder, ever wilder cries
Which shook the vault; but paced the room in
    thought.
"Must he be gagged?" he muttered; "it impedes
The action of the organs; with the gag
He will not last so long; but I foresee
His unfamiliar and articulate yells,
Will make my hand unsteady; will distract
My mind in ticklish moments, and defeat
My nicest observations;—shall I cut

His vocal organs? That hath objections too,
Which on the whole are greater." And he took
A gag from out a case.

                    But with a roar,
Like some wild beast, the captive bit his hand
Just as he placed the gag upon his mouth.
The pain was great, it made him clench his teeth,
And stand one moment helpless; but what made
His brow contract was pain alone, not wrath.
No word escaped him, and his face put on,
Almost at once, his former look again,
Inexorably placid. He resumed
The process with more caution. When 'twas o'er,
And not a sound could pass the captive's lips;
He washed his bitten hand and bound it up;
And as he did so muttered to himself:
"'Tis lucky 'tis the left; his teeth are sharp;
He bites, he bites; methinks he almost barked.
Oh, who shall draw the line betwixt this man,
This human animal, who nothing knows
Of what makes man immortal, and this dog?
That he can shriek for mercy? and the dog,
Hath he not shrieked for mercy long and loud?
That he can call on an unhelpful God?
So doth the dog perchance, if we but knew.
That he hath got a soul? I doubt it much;

But granting for a moment that he hath,
He's by so much the luckier than the dog,
Who suffers and relapses into nought.
O Prejudice, if I did let thee speak,
And stop my hand on this auspicious day,
When I can verify the work of years,
I were not what I am. Ay, ay, 'tis well
That 'twas the left he bit. Ye little dream,
Ye proud protected slaves who dub me quack
How soon ye shall be humbled. Have a care,
Fallopius, thou that thinkest thou art safe,
Because the Tuscan Duke gives thee alone
Live convicts to dissect. A man like me
Finds other ways. So crow not overloud:
My day at last has come."

    He then approached
Once more the table where his victim lay;
Surveyed him for a while, and felt his pulse;
Then raised his eyes towards the hole through
  which
The scanty light descended, falling straight
Upon the naked body, and began
To pace the cellar slowly up and down;
Probably waiting for the light to grow
As morning should advance. No sound was heard
Except the measured creaking of his step;

And through the tight compression of the gag
The other's stifled breathing—up and down
And up and down. At first no sign betrayed
The workings of his mind—but by-and-bye,
Just like a laden cloud about to burst,
Which ever and anon lets slip a flash;
He, laden with excitement long repressed,
Gave vent to muttered words with flashing eye
And rapid gestures, till at last his thoughts
Poured forth coherent though he spoke them low
And hurriedly, as if before some judge
Whom he alone could see, and who, to hear
Needed no louder pleading. "Who forbids?
Who dares to step between this deed and me?
'Tis God, perchance? Then let him first restrain
The dark destructive forces he has made:
First let him order that the deep no more
Shall every year engulf a thousand crews;
First let him chain the whirlwind or appease
The tiger's inborn rage, and put an end
To Nature's countless crimes.—Or is it Man
And Man alone? He strews his battle-fields
Year after year with heaps of mangled dead,
Without a why or wherefore; he doth let
His inconvenient rivals rot away
In dungeon cells, that he may sleep at ease,
Or roll in wealth and power. Shall he dare

" . . . . . Who forbids?"
Page 120.

To grudge me what I need—a single life
For Science, for the only thing I love
On this wide earth? And do I not deserve
To be at last rewarded? I whose life
Has been one boundless sacrifice—whose sight
Is prematurely dim from midnight work;
Whose back is bent from stooping o'er this work-
 board;
Whose youth knew nought of pleasure, but was
 spent
In solitary study, in the track
Of war and plague and famine, and where'er
Disease and death were teachers; and whose prime
Has gone in seeking knowledge in the corpse,
And in live dogs. Yea, did I not begin
By trampling with a firm relentless foot
On my own nature, making nerves as weak
As any woman's, stand the sight of things
From which the sickened hangman, growing pale,
Would turn away? Is there a risk,
However great, which I have feared to run
To get the bodies which the law refused?
Have I not snatched the newly-buried dead
And braved the dread resentment of despair,
Of mourning lovers and of outraged sons?
Have I not prowled at midnight with the wolf
About the gallows, where, had I been caught,

I should myself have dangled? Year by year
Have I not, thief-like, skulked from town to town,
From land to land, pursued with stones and jeers,
Until the very houses seemed to hoot
As I slunk by? And such a life as mine
Is to be cheated of its sole reward,
To save the squeaks of such a thing as *this*,
Which thinks not, reads not, writes not, knoweth
    nought
Of noble speculations, and but cares
For sunshine and for nutting in the woods,
Like any squirrel? Granted, he's a man:
But in his vitals lies concealed the drop
Of knowledge which I thirst for with a thirst
More irresistible than is the lust
For woman, or for power, or for gold.
Is not all Nature framed upon the plan
Of strength devouring weakness? Shall I be
More kind than Nature? He is in mine hands;
And mine is his existence by the right
Of paramount intelligence and power;
And if Mankind should ever learn this deed,
Would it avenge it for the victim's sake,
Or from its own intolerable fear
Of a like fate? Would it avenge the dog
Who lies on yonder table? O Mankind,
Thy charity is great!—And now to work.

THE DEATH OF THE DUCHESS ISABELLA.

"NOW have half of the kisses been given:
Fifty remain: one at morn, one at even,
Oh how slowly the sand in the time-glass slips,
Till at sunset again I shall touch its lips."

"*Mistress, sweet Mistress, beware, oh beware,*
Kiss not the portrait, nor mutter the prayer,
Cease while 'tis time, for it hideth a snare."

"Hush, little handmaid, and fear not the spell;
The Ducal Astrologer loveth me well,
When I have counted the last, not before,
Will the Duke seek my chamber and love me once more."

"*Oh Mistress, refrain; since these kisses began,*
Thy hand has grown thin, and thy cheek has grown wan,
Oh much I mistrust both the spell and the man."

"Hush, little maid, if my looks are such,
'Tis from loss of his love and from weeping o'er-
    much;
If my hand is thin, 'tis from chafe and fret,
That the hundredth kiss is so distant yet."

"*Duchess, sweet Duchess, oh let me speak;
Little thou knowest how changed is thy cheek,
Evil will come of this sinister freak.*"

"Give me the mirror. 'Tis strange, very strange,
What can account at my years for the change?
For my features, though pale, are as youthful as
    ever,
Give me the scissors; this lock I must sever."

"*She sees what I've noticed since yesterday night,
And what secretly fills me with grief and with
    fright:
Her tresses of gold at the roots have turned white.*

 .   .   .   .

"The sixtieth kiss will to-night be complete.
Oh the lips of the picture are passing sweet;
But sweeter his own; and soon he will shower,
These kisses all back; as in love's first hour."

*" Oh kiss it no more ; for strange stories are told,
About the Astrologer: death has he sold ;
Well is it known that he lives but for gold.*

" Oh, my hot head splits, and I fain would sleep,
The wings of these moments are clipped: they creep.
Unfasten my ruff: it is over-starched,
Give me to drink ; for my throat is parched."

.   .   .   .

(" *Her eyes look strange, with dark circles beneath*),
Oh Mistress, dost know that with bated breath,
Men whisper the Duke is resolved on thy death ? "

" That well might be, for he loves me not now,
But the hundredth kiss will regain him, I trow,
A harlot hath stolen his heart away,
The sixty-ninth kiss hath been given to-day."

" *The Duke and the Alchemist deep in the wood,
Were met by my brother, who ill understood
That which they said ; but it boded no good.*"

" Thy brother deserves the severest rebuke,
For spreading such tales : miles away is the Duke,
Give me to drink. (Oh that horrible pain,
Like the stab of a knife has pierced me again)."

"*Mistress, sweet Mistress, desist, oh desist,
Never again must the picture be kissed,
Wilt thou thy handmaid's entreaties resist?*"

. . . .

" Help me to walk to the picture. Not yet,
Alas, may I kiss it! the sun has not set.
Yes, thou art right; I am ill, very ill;
But not from the kisses. They're twenty-nine still."

"*There hangs all about it a strange sickly taint;
And the canvas shines through, where the lips have
    grown faint:
Her seventy kisses have eaten the paint.*"

" Tell me, my handmaid? didst never behold
The woman he loves? Has she tresses of gold,
As long and as wavy, as glossy and fine,
Or fingers as white and as tapered as mine?"

"*How should I see her? To thee I am tied;
But much I have heard of her insolent pride,
As if she were Duchess she rides by his side.*"

" Let her exult, till the hundredth kiss
Between their two hearts shall create an abyss!
And then let her learn, when of love she is robbed
To sob in the twilight as oft I have sobbed."

"*She thinks of nought else. Ah that portrait accursed,
How quick I would burn it if only I durst,
But I shrink from the terrible storm that would burst.*"

. . . .

"Give me thy hand; let me lean on thy shoulder,
My limbs, though 'tis August, grow colder and colder,
And the cold of my feet rises higher and higher,
But give me to drink, my throat is on fire.

"*The water she asks for would float a ship,
But when holding the glass she can scarcely sip,
All swollen and black is her nether lip.*"

"Pray open the window; a sweet breeze is sighing,
Dost know, little maiden? I think I am dying;
If only I reach to the hundredth and see
His face on the threshold, death painless will be.

"*Oh speak not of dying, my Duchess dear,
Thy body is fevered, but death is not near.
(I feel, though I hide it, a horrible fear.*")

"A song of my childhood, a beautiful song,
Runs in my head; but the words are all wrong,

"'The wren in her nest, and the mouse in his hole,'
It's something like that: no, I think it's the mole."

"'*The robin and wren have new feathered their nest;
And the dormouse and mole in new velvet are drest;*'
*That's the song, is it not? Shall I sing thee the
   rest?*"

Mark how the clouds on the sunset are drifting!
I see many faces perpetually shifting;
There's the head of the Duke: how they move,
   how they move!
It has changed to a wolf. Is't a wolf that I love?"

"*Methinks that she wanders, as rageth her fever;
The thought of the Duke not one moment doth leave
   her,
On the number of kisses I'll try to deceive her.*"

"Thou liest. The number is seventy-seven,
The seventy-eighth will at sunset be given,
My head grows enormous, nor ceases to swell,
More water, more water. I think this is Hell."

"*Each moment more desperate groweth her state,
The leech that I sent for, appears not; 'tis late,
'Tis clear he's been stopped by the guard at the gate.*

"Help me across to the picture: the sun,
Approaches the level; its journey is done,
Hold me securely, or else I shall fall;
The floor seems to stagger—I'll hold to the wall."

"*Oh Mistress, sweet Mistress, dost hear me entreat,
Thou seest, no more can'st thou keep on thy feet,
Oh do not that kiss of damnation repeat!*"

"Where is the Picture? my sight is grown dim,
My senses uncertain, and all things swim,
Look at the sun; let me know when it dips,
Where are the lips of the picture, the lips?"

"*My Mistress, sweet Mistress, oh take to your bed.
She falls, and her body is heavy as lead,
Help, help! Is there no one? The Duchess is dead!*"

THE END.

S. Cowan & Co., Strathmore Press, Perth.

NEW BOOKS

PUBLISHED BY

Messrs. W. SATCHELL & Co.

Now Ready, Royal 8°, *cloth, Price* 14s. (*Postage* 8½d.)

STUDIES OF THE EIGHTEENTH CENTURY IN ITALY.

By VERNON LEE.

CONTENTS.

THE ARCADIAN ACADEMY—THE MUSICAL LIFE—METASTASIO AND THE OPERA—THE COMEDY OF MASKS—GOLDONI AND THE REALISTIC COMEDY—CARLO GOZZI AND THE VENETIAN FAIRY COMEDY.

"Mr. Vernon Lee, if that be the author's real name, has written one of the most fascinating books that it has been our good fortune to meet with for a very long time." .... "A singularly delightful and very able volume."—*Westminster Review.*

"These studies show a wide range of knowledge of the subject, precise investigation, abundant power of illustration, and healthy enthusiasm. .... The style of writing is cultivated, neatly adjusted, and markedly clever; it has a certain analogy to the styles of some other aesthetic writers of the day, combining (we might say by way of indication) something of Mr. Wedmore and of Mrs. Pattison, with a spice of Mr. Pater, and another spice of Mr. Swinburne. .... On the whole, it can be cordially recommended as treating an important and little known theme with conspicuous ability."—*Athenæum*, June 12.

"The story of the birth and life of the Arcadian Academy is a curious one. . . It is told in a . . . . style both interesting and amusing. .... A sketch given of the state of society in Italy at this period is clever and readable. Much detail in musical and dramatic matters may be pleasantly learned from other parts of Vernon Lee's volume.—*Saturday Review,* June 26.

"Mr. Lee has brought to his subject a great amount of curious and recondite learning. The 'Arcadian Academy' is a thing wholly unknown to the vast majority of readers. . . . Mr Lee gives a curious picture of its constitution and proceedings, and brings out clearly before our eyes a strange phase of literary life. His fourth and sixth essays, dealing respectively with 'Metastasio and the Opera,' and 'Goldoni and the Realistic Comedy,' brings us into more familiar regions, and are, we are bound to say, far more interesting. The sketch of Metastasio's life is particularly worthy of remark. Mr. Lee throws plenty of vigour and colour into his portraiture. His style . . . . has a certain robustness; while his criticism is often just and even subtle.—*Spectator,* June 26.

Now ready, Fcap. 4º, Cloth, gilt. Price 7s. 6d. (Postage 8d.)

THE ANGLER'S NOTE-BOOK AND NATURALIST'S RECORD. A Repertory of fact, inquiry, and discussion on Field-Sports and subjects of Natural History. With six illustrations on plate paper. The *Green* Series complete.

CONTENTS: "The Oldest English Treatise on Fishing," and "Anglo-Saxon Fish-Names," by the Rev. Professor Skeat; "An Unknown Angling Poet," "One of the Mysteries of Angling Literature," Conrad Heresbach; "Concerning Fishing" (a translation of his *De piscatione*), &c., by Thomas Westwood, author of the *Bibliotheca Piscatoria;* "Fishing Cats," &c., by William Henderson; "Invitation to Coquet," by Joseph Crawhall, editor of "Newcastle Fishers' Garlands;" "Fishing a Scotch Loch," by the Rev. M. G. Watkins; "Notes from the Journals of Jonathan Couch," and several hundred papers and short notes—in prose and verse—by many other well-known writers and naturalists.

"Wading through its pages is like wading up a Devonshire trout-stream, at every turn there is something interesting to note and store away in the angler's memory."—*Fishing Gazette.*
"Brimful of eminently readable matter."—*Nottingham Paper.*
"We strongly recommend it to all anglers and lovers of nature generally."—*Bath Journal.*
"Has attained a high position." "An admirable publication."—*Civilian.*

Now ready, Imp. 16º, elegant cover, gilt. Price 3s 6d. (Postage 4d.)

TUSCAN FAIRY TALES. Taken down from the mouths of the people. With sixteen illustrations, engraved by Edmund Evans.

CONTENTS: The little Convent of Cats; The Fairies' Sieve; The Three Golden Apples; The Woman of Paste; The Beautiful Glutton; The King of Portugal's Cowherd; The Three Cauliflowers; The Siren; The Glass Coffin; Leonbruno.

"Sumptuously printed and prettily bound"—*Athenæum.*

Imp. 4º, in handsome cloth cover, Price Three Guineas.

A QUAINT TREATISE ON "FLEES AND THE ART A' ARTYFICHALL FLEE MAKING," by an old man well known on the Derbyshire streams a century ago; printed from an old MS. never before published. The original spelling and language being retained, with editorial notes, patterns of flies and samples of the materials for making each fly.

By W. H. ALDAM.

With two fac-similes of water-colour drawings by James Poole.

"None but a perfect enthusiast could have conceived and carried out so remarkable a work as this. Since Dame Juliana Berners wrote her 'Treatyse of Fyshing wyth an Angle,' no work so remarkable has issued from the press upon this subject... The illustrations are... the actual flies themselves, dressed by Mr. Aldam himself and 'by two of the most accomplished fly-tyers in the kingdom.'... Every two or three pages or so, in this book, there is a thick cardboard page, in which are two counter-sunk oval medallions; and here you have, first the fly, below it the silk it is tied with, and the harl, floss, or dubbing for the body; on one side is the feather from which the wings are made; on the other, the hackle for the legs."—*Field.*

"No verbal description can convey the idea of shades of colour; but the student of fly-making has the colours and materials themselves before him."—*The Times.*

"Fly-fishers will be delighted with this book."—*Standard.*

"Those who are fond of fly-fishing should obtain a copy of this handsome and most useful work, which is not only interesting to anglers, but also to the public in general who admire perseverance, taste, and first-class workmanship."—FRANK BUCKLAND.—*Land and Water.*

"As a Work of Art this 'Treatise' stands unrivalled in the peculiar class of literature of which it forms a portion."—*Sheffield Daily Telegraph.*

"One of the most elegant and unique works pertaining to the art of angling ever produced. The book, with its stores, is a grand contribution to angling literature."—*Once a Week.*

Medium 8vo, Price 12s., *xvii and* 329 *pages.* (*Postage* 9d).

THE FOLK-LORE OF THE NORTHERN COUNTIES OF ENGLAND AND THE BORDERS. A new edition, with many additional notes.

By WILLIAM HENDERSON,
Author of "My Life as an Angler."

CONTENTS : Customs at Birth, Marriage, and Death ; and on particular Days and Seasons. Spells and Divinations. Portents and Auguries. The Gabriel Hounds and the Wild Huntsmen. Charms and Spells. Witchcraft—Drawing blood from Witches—Witch hunting—Witch riding; Witches in the Dairy; Wizards ; The Evil Eye ; Incantations. Divining by Bible and Key. The Hand of Glory. Spirits ; Bogles, Brownies, Dobies, Dunters, Hobs, Pegs, Pouries, Redcaps, Cauld Lads, Silkies, &c., &c. Worms or Dragons ; The Sockburn Worm ; The Pollard Worm ; The Lambton Worm ; the Laidley Worm of Spindleston Haugh ; Dragons at St.. Osyth's, &c. Origin of these Legends. Occult Powers and Sympathies : Seventh Sons—Aerial appearances—Bees and their owners, &c. Haunted Houses. Haunted mines. The Willington Ghost. The Sexhow Farmer and old Nannie. The old Lady of Littledean. Apparition in Fifeshire. A Devon Legend. Sussex Ghosts, &c., &c. Dreams presaging Death. Discovering bodies. Visions. The Bodach Glas. Second Sight, &c., &c.

"We congratulate the Folk-Lore Society on the new edition of this excellent book."—*Athenæum.*

"The new and enlarged edition of an old favourite, the work of 'a folk-lore student before folk-lore came into vogue as a pursuit,' cannot fail to be welcome to the large and increasing number of students who make this interesting subject their principal pursuit. We have here a mass of material, the accumulation of years of search and inquiry."—*Notes and Queries.*

"So largely increased by important and valuable additions as to be virtually a new book. . . . No mere dry compilation, but a store of delightful entertainment which is well nigh inexhaustible. An index after Mr. Carlyle's own heart has been furnished, with great labour and thought, by Mr. Thomas Satchell, to whom the volume thus owes an augmentation of utility."—*Daily Telegraph.*

THE BOOK

OF

BRITISH TOPOGRAPHY:

A CLASSIFIED CATALOGUE OF THE
TOPOGRAPHICAL BOOKS IN THE LIBRARY OF
THE BRITISH MUSEUM RELATING TO
GREAT BRITAIN AND IRELAND.

BY JOHN P. ANDERSON,

OF THE MUSEUM LIBRARY.

PROSPECTUS.

THE great and abiding interest with which the English-speaking races regard the localities in these islands that are associated with historical events, with famous men, or with their own immediate ancestry, precludes the necessity of any apology for the issue of a work which provides a safe and comprehensive guide to the vast collection of Topographical books relating to Great Britain and Ireland, by far the most complete existing, now preserved in the Library of the British Museum.

The urgent need of a work of this character had long been felt, both by the frequenters of the Museum Reading Room, and by those who, living at a distance, wish to learn what books the National Library contains relating to the places in which they are personally interested.

Upcott's excellent Catalogue (1818) is at present the most recent available for reference, if we except that included in the Catalogue of the Hoare Library at Stourhead (1840), and that printed by the late John Camden Hotten.

During the sixty years that have passed since the publication of Upcott's Catalogue, a large number of works have been written upon British Topography, many of them being valuable county histories, and others of much local importance.

Apart from its utility, this most recent addition to bibliographical literature will be found interesting from the fact that it is the first Classified Catalogue ever published of books in the Library of the British Museum.

The work, upon which the author has been engaged for many years, and which could scarcely have been accomplished by any person unconnected with the Library, includes Scotland and Ireland, hitherto much neglected by the bibliographer, and will contain about 13,000 entries, brought down to the present date, with ample indices of persons and places.

The numerous local Directories in the Library, invaluable for elucidating family history and descent, have been for the first time included in a work of this character.

The following arrangement has been adopted :—

The books relating generally to Great Britain, to Great Britain and Ireland, to England, to Wales, to Scotland, and to Ireland, are arranged according to the nature of their contents under various sub-headings.

The books relating to particular Counties are arranged alphabetically under the places or localities in each, and in chronological order as far as practicable.

To facilitate the labour of referring to the Museum Catalogues, the heading under which each book will be found therein, is indicated by conspicuous type in every title, a saving of time and patience, especially in the case of anonymous works, which can be best estimated by those who are under the constant necessity of using the 2000 MS. volumes, of which the Museum Catalogue now consists.

The work will be finely printed in clear type on good paper, and issued to subscribers at 15s per copy. A limited number of copies will also be printed for sale to the public at 21s per copy.

www.ingramcontent.com/pod-product-compliance
Lightning Source LLC
Chambersburg PA
CBHW030302170426
43202CB00009B/843